From Acorns...

PEARSON
Prentice Hall
BUSINESS

Books that make you better

Books that make you better. That make you *be* better, *do* better, *feel* better. Whether you want to upgrade your personal skills or change your job, whether you want to improve your managerial style, become a more powerful communicator, or be stimulated and inspired as you work.

Prentice Hall Business is leading the field with a new breed of skills, careers and development books. Books that are a cut above the mainstream – in topic, content and delivery – with an edge and verve that will make you better, with less effort.

Books that are as sharp and smart as you are.

Prentice Hall Business.
We work harder – so you don't have to.

For more details on products, and to contact us, visit
www.pearsoned.co.uk
www.yourmomentum.com

From Acorns...

... how to build your brilliant business from scratch

by Caspian Woods

an imprint of Pearson Education
London • New York • Toronto • Sydney • Tokyo • Singapore •
Hong Kong • Cape Town • New Delhi • Madrid • Paris
• Amsterdam • Munich • Milan

PEARSON EDUCATION LIMITED
Head Office:
Edinburgh Gate
Harlow CM20 2JE
Tel: +44 (0) 1279 623623
Fax: +44 (0) 1279 431059

First published in Great Britain in 2004

British Library Cataloguing-in-Publication Data
A catalogue record for this book is available from the British Library

Concept and design by Editions Publishing
Visit us at: www.editions.co.uk

Cartoon illustrations by Bill Piggins (pp.8, 48, 90, 93, 100, 117, 138, 146, and 150)

Printed and bound by Bell & Bain Ltd, Glasgow

The publisher's policy is to use paper manufactured from sustainable forests.

Dedicated to Ruth Simpson

Contents

Acknowledgements

My special thanks to:

Rachael Stock for being a truly entrepreneurial publisher.

Julie (and Scarlett and Felix) for putting up with my late nights and not trying to eat my laptop while I worked.

My dad for giving me the support, encouragement and freedom to go and try to do whatever I wanted to, and Patricia for the creative input and for providing a writing refuge in Southwold.

Sandy Paton, for expert input and guidance, and for walking the walk.

Our design team: Jane Greig, Davy Thomson and Vicky Allen – for resisting the urge to politely tell me where to go and stick my 'creative suggestions'. Elizabeth Steele and Nan Tulloch, for watching the fort.

Ray Perman, a true publishing entrepreneur, for giving me an early break and for leaving me a card that said 'you have talent and will go far' – which has kept me going when things are hard.

Suzy Hamilton for design inspiration.

And Paul Welham for allowing me to slander him, and for the brilliant design suggestions (except the ones with my dodgy eye).

A big thank you to our partners in this book:

Pearson: The very dapper Peter Smith and his cracking team, and Richard Stagg, Caroline Wheeler and Julie Knight.

Bank of Scotland: Tom Abraham, Moray Watson and the team for their support

Prince's Scottish Youth Business Trust: Mark Strudwick, Carol Anne McMahon and the team, for helping me start in business, and continued support.

Scottish Enterprise: Terrie Currie and Robin Mair, for their support on this project, and for years of work that have made the term 'entrepreneur' a compliment.

The top ten tips

1. Get selling

Business is not rocket science. If you've got plenty of people buying things from you for more than they cost you, you are most of the way there.

There are many distractions along the way, but you should always be spending *at least* 50 per cent of your time selling.

2. Strive to be different

There is a lot of noise out there, and a lot of big boring companies and products. Genuine original thinking does not cost a penny, and with a bit of it you can really leap ahead of the competition.

3. Don't take rejection personally

You are going to get a lot of knock-backs in business – the secret is not to let them get you down. As any nightclub Casanova will tell you – success is a numbers game (see page 91).

4. Cash is king - hire a dragon

You haven't sold anything until the cash is in your bank. Lack of cash in your bank can bust even the brightest business. Hire a dragon to keep control of it (see page 117).

5. Cost your own time properly

Your business's scarcest resource? It's your time. Only spend it on the areas where you add the most value. Also, cost your own time properly – you might be willing to work for 50p an hour, but you will never be able to find anyone else who will.

6. Raise your price...

...and keep increasing it until your customers begin to squeak. Remember, the right price is what your customers are willing to pay. Your costs only tell you if you've got a good deal from your suppliers.

7. Get out of engine room and on to the bridge

Don't spend weeks lovingly crafting an intricate business plan then dump it in a drawer. Take time out regularly to think about the direction of your business, even if your plans are scribbled on the back of an envelope.

8. Get a mentor

Starting in business can be like climbing a mountain in flip-flops with only a road map to guide you. Why not get the advice of someone who has been there before?

9. Bear in mind, sometimes customers don't want the best - they want the least worst

A prime factor in winning and keeping customers is reassurance. This feeling of trust comes from having a good brand. To build a good brand, you don't need big bucks.

10. Be persistent and avoid isolation

Our greatest glory is not in never falling; it is in rising every time we fall. Surround yourself with supporters so you keep your mojo even when things are bad.

Foreword

Small and medium-sized businesses are the lifeblood of the UK's economy. They now employ more people and generate a greater share of the national wealth than the public sector and large companies.

There is also now a greater recognition of the people who start their own businesses and of the challenges they face. According to the Government's Household survey, over three quarters of the population would encourage family and friends to start their own enterprise.

At Bank of Scotland, we have always understood their importance and that every business is unique. We also appreciate that the people who want to run their own business are as different as the population at large in terms of age, gender and ethnic background.

We are at the forefront of breaking the mould in business banking by being the first to introduce concepts such as the choice for the customer of potentially free banking and paying interest on current accounts as standard. We aim to improve the deal that businesses get from their bank and provide specialist guidance and support for ambitious entrepreneurs from all backgrounds as they grow from small acorns to entrepreneurial oaks like Tom Hunter.

We are therefore delighted to support this guide. It aims to highlight the issues you need to consider and simplify the process you need to go through to start and build a brilliant business. It also passes on the wisdom of many entrepreneurs who have been there before. If you would like more support, we would be delighted to hear from you. Visit us online at: **www.bankofscotland.co.uk/business/startup** or call us on: **0845 850 0582** (Type Talk available) quoting 'From Acorns' to see how we could help you.

Good luck!

Tom Abraham

Managing Director, Bank of Scotland Corporate Banking

Preface

When you start out in business, you feel like the smallest acorn. You look around at the business oaks and find it impossible to imagine that they were once as small as you. You forget that the largest companies in the world started from bedrooms, market stalls and backs of vans.

Business is not rocket science, but many guides treat it as if it is. This book is not a technical manual. Rather, it is an attempt to show how simple starting up is by passing on the tips, nuggets of wisdom and inspiration from countless entrepreneurs young and old.

This is also built very much on my own experience. I have started and run a succession of businesses, such as an event organiser called 'Let me hold your balls for you', a magazine I launched by living in a shop window for a week surviving solely off the internet, and my current custom publishing business, Editions. When I talk about the importance of having a hangover to come up with good ideas or crying as a negotiating technique, I'm speaking from experience.

But I'm keenest to prove that entrepreneurship is open to anyone. As my best friend Paul commented, 'The Caspian I grew up with couldn't spot a gap in the pavement, let alone a gap in the market'. Don't be put-off by the born hustlers we see on our TVs. The real success stories are the millions of people who are quietly living their dreams around the country.

I hope you enjoy the book, and find that it helps. I would very much like to know your feedback, hints and opinions so that I can share them with other budding entrepreneurs in the future.

You can email me at: **caspian@fromacorns.com**
Good luck!
Caspian Woods

Join the *From Acorns* community

One of the greatest causes of small business failure is isolation.

To overcome this, we have set up a community for those starting and building brilliant businesses. By logging on, you will get access to:

- Tools to support this book such as form and templates
- Further information and links for building your business.
- The chance to give feedback and swap stories.

Simply visit at **www.fromacorns.com** .

How we can all make Britain more entrepreneurial

In our hands, we have the power to make Britain entrepreneurial. There is one thing we must do for its small businesses. We must

Patronise them

I mean this of course in the old sense of the word. The best thing you can give a small business is your custom. Whenever you have a choice in supplier, always try to use the smaller entrepreneurial one:

- This is good for the business – they get growth
- This is good for you – you get a highly motivated supplier
- It is good for the country as a whole.

CHAPTER 1

Oaks from small acorns grow...

Oaks from small acorns grow...

Some years ago, a young entrepreneur called Marcus Samuel set up a small shop in the East End of London. He spotted a growing craze for seashells, partly for decoration, and partly for natural history enthusiasts. He set about specialising in this market.

After a while, and being an enterprising type of chap, he soon realised he could make more money from actually shipping the shells in from the Far East and selling them to other shops. The Marcus Samuel Shipping and Trading Company was born.

On a business trip there, his son spotted that there was also an abundance of oil which they could ship at the same time, and built a special boat for this. The year was 1890, and the company changed its name, in recognition of its main cargo, to the Shell Transport and Trading Company. As the demand for oil really took off and replaced the shells, the company became good old Shell Oil.

Shell is today the largest retailer in the world.

The moral of this story? Every business starts as an acorn. Yet, when you are taking your first baby steps into business, it is far too easy to be daunted by the vast business oaks that seem to surround you.

Well, don't be. Take a look at a cross-section of the household names of today: Marks & Spencer, Monsoon, Microsoft, JP Morgan. They started from market stalls, bedrooms, barrows and backs of vans.

Everyone has to start somewhere, but with a bit of risk, and a lot of determination, the sky really is the limit.

CHAPTER 2

Is it *really* for you?

Is it *really* for you?

Before you launch yourself headlong into your new business venture, it's important to know what you are letting yourself in for.

It is very tempting to look at the self-employed and think – 'Ah the lucky people, they don't have a boss, they can work whenever they want, they have flunkeys to do all the dirty work, and yet they get paid loads of money'.

There are certainly lots of benefits to being self-employed, and we'll come on to those. But first, let's be realistic about the costs.

The downside

- **Risk:** Risk and reward go hand in hand in a new business. Most people just get hung-up on the worry of financial risk.

  However, the greatest fear you will have to overcome is the risk of being seen to fail, of 'friends' and competitors saying 'I told you so', and the possible dent to your self-esteem. This is usually just a fear of the unknown. If you want to know what failure is really like – turn to Chapter 23 all about the different types of failure.
- **Hard work:** Without doubt, running your business in the early days will be harder than working for someone else. Quite often your family, your friends and your social life will come a poor second to your new business. You have to be sure that this is the right time in your life to be making this type of commitment.
- **Responsibility:** In your own business the buck stops with you. Unfortunately, it also has a tendency to follow you home at night. If you are the kind of person who lies in bed worrying at night about the government's exchange rate policy, or whether the

neighbour's tree is encroaching on your garden, then think hard about the added worries that running your own business will bring you.

Timing is vital for small business success. If you are not sure this is the right moment for you, then don't worry. Keep your dreams bubbling away and your plans on ice until the right moment arrives to take the jump.

The upside

Of course, there are many benefits to running your own venture. Chief among these are:

Control over your own destiny: It is no coincidence that many entrepreneurs hate being told what to do. One of the major benefits of being self-employed is the chance to do things your own way, work your own hours, turn up to work in your pyjamas if the mood takes you. It sure beats working for someone you don't respect. Surprisingly, being self-employed can be a lot less stressful than working for someone else, and in this ever-changing world sometimes offers more job security.

A chance to prove yourself:

> I was with a group of entrepreneurs who were speaking at a schools' careers convention. We were asked how well we had done at school. It turned out that, without exception, we were all underachievers, drop-outs, slackers or day-dreamers. I still have the school report that says 'Caspian might achieve something if he woke up for five minutes and could remember where his books are'.

From meeting and interviewing many successful entrepreneurs, I have found that deep down they are often driven to prove themselves to others because of a strong feeling of personal inadequacy. This typically stems from a formative stage at childhood. Many entrepreneurs, like Richard Branson, are dyslexic, some moved to foreign countries at a young age, one was moved from a very smart private school to the rough comprehensive next door when his

father's business collapsed. Whatever the reasons, their endeavours certainly make the world a more interesting place.

A chance to create things: For many people, the greatest satisfaction is that of creating things from nothing or indulging in a passion. Getting paid to do this can almost seem like a wonderful bonus.

Money: Money is clearly a major part of the story. It was certainly the view of the mechanic fixing my car last week. 'Money doesn't buy you happiness,' I claimed. 'Hmm,' said the mechanic, 'my neighbour won £3million on the lottery and you couldn't have taken the smile off his face with a spanner.'

If you want to become seriously wealthy, then self-employment is probably the way to go. It is not so much that you can pay yourself whatever you want, it is the chance of perhaps selling out for millions.

However, I have put money deliberately at the bottom of the list. This is where it comes in many interviews with successful entrepreneurs. Almost without fail, their advice is:

 Follow your dreams first, and the money will come after

CHAPTER 3

Do I have what it takes?

Do I have what it takes?

What is an entrepreneur?

Most people's mental image of an entrepreneur is still Del Boy Trotter from *Only Fools and Horses*. There are still a few of these duckers and divers around. However, every detailed study of 'entrepreneurs' shows they comprise a huge range of people from shy scientists to shady car salesmen. On the surface, they have surprisingly little in common.

To get to the heart of what an entrepreneur is, or does, I think you have to dissect the definition. According to my *Collins English Dictionary*, 'entrepreneur' is from a nineteenth-century French word meaning 'to undertake'. The definition is:

entrepreneur: *n.* **1.** the owner of an enterprise who, by risk and initiative, attempts to make profits. [C19. from French, from *entreprendre* to undertake.]

'The owner of an enterprise...': Enterprise is much wider than a business. I would include explorers like Chris Bonnington, artists, many people working in the charity sector and, more and more, people being entrepreneurial within large companies. You could possibly stretch it to say 'the owner of a dream' if that didn't sound painfully new-agey.

More important are the two following characteristics:

'...who, by risk': The most fundamental economic equation is:

 Profit is the reward for risk

To be successful, you have to be prepared to take a risk.

The most obvious risk people think of is the financial one. But there is a bigger risk that people don't often admit to. It is a fear of failure. It is a fear of looking stupid, or of people saying, 'I told you so'. It is a fear, ultimately, of rejection.

This fear is possibly the greatest barrier to entrepreneurship in Britain.

> *My first entrepreneurial venture was to produce a yearbook for my final year at university. As you can perhaps imagine, it was pretty irreverent, with lots of compromising photos, a few rude words and lists of who everyone most wanted to snog. I invested about £1,000 I didn't have to print the books.*
>
> *So, along came graduation day. I set up a stall and stood there, smiling nervously, waiting to see if anyone would actually buy one of these. Instead, the first person to appear was an ancient cobweb-covered academic who shuffled out of nowhere like Herman Munster. He picked up the yearbook and thumbed through it while I watched nervously to see my first customer's reaction. He tossed it back on the desk and said, 'What complete rubbish. It is a disgrace to the university name, and I'm going to have it stopped.' He turned around and lumbered off.*
>
> *I never heard from or saw him again. The students piled in, and they bought (or more accurately, got their parents to buy) lots of the yearbooks, and I earned enough to pay the printers and get my first business off the ground.*
>
> *The point is, his comments really struck home. This was years ago, and I can still remember it clearly.*

There will always be people eager to stop you taking a risk – whether out of genuine concern, frustration, jealousy or ill-fitting pants. But if you care passionately about your venture, you must learn not to take things like this to heart. Chapter 4 gives you some tips about doing this.

'...and initiative...': Initiative, drive, enthusiasm, energy – this is the indispensable element of the entrepreneur. It is far more important than pure 'talent'. It is not how good you are that counts, it's how good you want to be.

This is the drive to start things. It may come from frustration, boredom, curiosity or a drive to prove yourself to others – these motivations are as diverse as the businesses they spawn.

But whatever the reason, drive and enthusiasm is the indispensable element of the entrepreneur, and without it, nothing great is ever achieved.

> *Sir Tom Farmer exemplifies this huge enthusiasm. As a schoolboy, he took a job in a local chemist rather than spending hours studying. He left school at 14 to work in the stores of a local tyre company during the day. In the evenings he started a cooker cleaning business to keep him busy. At the age of 23 he talked a bank into lending him £200 to start his own business. Four years later, he sold this for half a million pounds. He then set up the first of his Kwik-Fit outlets, which he ultimately sold for many millions.*

'...attempts to make profits': Not all entrepreneurs hang around used car lots in sheepskin coats counting out a thick bundle of grubby fivers.

Profit is vital for your business to grow. But most successful entrepreneurs are not motivated by money. Look at Richard Branson – you would think he has enough desert islands by now.

Ask most successful entrepreneurs, and they will tell you that they just did what they loved. The money came later.

So, are entrepreneurs born or can they be made?

Nothing seems to divide an audience more than this question, and thousands of hours of academic study must have gone into answering it. Here's my contribution:

There is no doubt that when you meet some of these archetypal entrepreneurs it is impossible to imagine them doing anything else. They were the ones who were told in primary school they would either end up in prison, or as a millionaire. They often end up doing both.

But beyond this minority of born hustlers, there is a huge variety of very successful entrepreneurs who certainly don't fit this mould. So, don't worry if you don't think you look the part, or you are allergic to sheepskin. If all you have is the enthusiasm to start something, and a willingness to take a bit of risk, then the world is yours for the taking.

What type of entrepreneur are you?

There are different types of entrepreneurs, though no one of them is the right type. Probably the ultimate goal is to have the financial freedom to do what you enjoy the most. This can come from an income of £6,000 or £600,000. However, it's essential you know from the outset what type of entrepreneur you are, as this will affect many of your business decisions.

Lifestyle entrepreneur: You want to earn a good standard of living for yourself, with control of your destiny, but no more beyond this. Many people use the term 'lifestyle' as a term of condescension. It's difficult to see why.

> 'John' is a graphic designer who specialises in whisky labels. His business consists of him, his old Volvo and his Labrador. However, he has an international reputation, he commands great fees for his work, he gets the satisfaction of seeing his work around the world, and can pick and choose when and where he works.

If this sums up your approach, then bear in mind the following challenges you might face:

- Your most precious resource is your time. While you will probably be keen not to take on and manage staff, bear in mind how a few of the right supporters can take a huge amount of your non-productive work off your shoulders. See Chapter 5 for information on time management.
- You will have to price your time accurately and learn to say 'no' to the wrong type of work.
- Isolation will be a risk for you. Make sure you have a good network of supporters. See Chapter 24.

- You will probably have fewer clients, so nurturing strong relationships with them is essential. See Chapter 17.

Empire builder: Your fascination is growth. You may not know what business this will be in, just so long as you can grow it. Your role model is likely to be Citizen Kane. Though money will need to feature in the growth of your income, your dreams are probably more about being applauded onto a podium.

- For you, the most important challenge is your initial idea. You have to think long and hard to find a business that has strong growth potential (see Chapter 6).
- You will need to ensure that someone is watching the cashflow, tax and legals because these bits will get in the way of sales.
- You will have to ensure that you are continually planning (Chapter 18), as your path will change many times in your career.
- You will have to build a good team around you of people who are better at their jobs than you are, to make sure that you can deliver your dreams.

Social entrepreneur: You have probably never thought of yourself as an entrepreneur. You are certainly not doing it for the money. However, you have a strong desire to bring your vision to fruition, whether it is opening an art gallery, taking a group of disadvantaged youngsters to Disneyland, or changing a particularly unjust piece of legislation.

You are just as much an entrepreneur as the others, and there is plenty here you can learn from.

The intrapreneur: This is someone who sets up a business under the wing of their current employer. They don't own all of the company, but have a degree of reward linked to performance. Purists get very touchy about this 'they aren't entrepreneurs – they have no risk'. Well, if aim of the entrepreneur is get the maximum reward for the minimum risk, you cannot really fault the canny intrapreneur who gets the company to underwrite their risk for them.

Ajaz Ahmed joined Dixons as a shop-floor worker at 16 on £30 a week. He was determined to be rich. He bought a computer and was amazed no one could tell him how to connect to the internet. He pestered his bosses that they had to be the first company to help get their customers online, which eventually led to the foundation of Freeserve. The company grew and at one stage was worth more than Dixons itself. When it was sold for £1.6bn, although a minority shareholder, Ajaz Ahmed still made a good deal of money.

CHAPTER 4

How to become a better risk-taker

How to become a better risk-taker

Being a risk-taker is vital, whether in business, or just in life. You must learn to set no limits on where you could possibly end up.

Being a better risk-taker will affect everything from product design, your sales and marketing, and the journey you take.

We think our tolerance for risk is something we are born with, but it is never too late to learn to increase your tolerance for risk. The following are two exercises:

Kill the McTaggarts of Dundee!

I was consulting with the chief executive of a computer company. He was a guy you could listen to all night. He was full of anecdotes about the early days of computing, sharing beers with Bill Gates, and setting up early satellite systems. But when we looked at his company's image and products they were all a little tired, dull and run of the mill.

I asked him, 'Why don't you put more of your passion and originality into your business?' He replied, 'Well, we have a client called [let's call them 'McTaggarts of Dundee']. They are a family run firm and have been around for generations. We have to be serious for them and present in suits and ties or they won't use us.'

They let the McTaggarts of Dundee dictate the business to the other 99 per cent of their customer base.

The problem is, we all have these McTaggarts of Dundee.

They might be clients who have criticised us, friends who secretly resent us for being more successful than they are, parents who don't want us to get hurt, teachers at school who were blinkered, spouses worried about the mortgage.

The problem is that we listen to them and accept their limitations. They stop us thinking and acting passionately and effectively. They stop us being different and creative, and entrepreneurial. So, we must kill them. OK, not literally, but through the following steps.

Toolkit: Silence your critics by using this grid and the steps overleaf:

The McTaggart	Situation	What behaviour	Evidence	Their reason
Example: Head of marketing at blue-chip firm	A cold call I made	I felt I didn't have a compelling enough offer	Not really	He gets 30 cold calls a day and is extremely busy

Column 1: You need to draw up a list of who your possible McTaggarts are. You might know some instantly. To work out the others, try asking the following questions:

- Who has laughed at a recent idea of mine, or told me not to do something I really wanted to?
- If I were on a podium delivering a speech and I forgot my words, who would I most hate to see in that audience?
- Think of your wildest dream. Who would I be most embarrassed to admit this to?
- If I were to turn up in a Porsche – who would be the most jealous?
- Think back to particular pieces of criticism you got as a child or at school. Who said them?

Column 3: Look through each person in column 1 and ask yourself, what aspect of your personality or behaviour was criticised or embarrassed you the most?

Column 4: Just a simple tick or cross. Has the person in column 1 ever made the criticism in column 2 explicit, or have you just assumed it?

Column 5: What might it be about *their* personality or circumstances that might cause your McTaggarts to criticise you?

Hopefully you are now some way towards identifying and eliminating your McTaggarts. You should start to realise some things:

1. They account for only 1 per cent of our possible audience.
2. In many cases, we have never asked them! We have assumed they would criticise us. Chances are, they are the ones who would most applaud us.
3. There are possibly some valid criticisms in here, but this is a part of our rounded personalities. Good starters tend not to be good finishers for example.
4. Their dependence on us, jealousy, embarrassment, or frustration more often fuels their criticism rather than anything we have done.

Become an immigrant: It is no coincidence that many successful entrepreneurs through history and across countries are immigrants. The reason? They have no history in their new country. They can break all the rules, makes lots of mistakes and not have their neighbours looking over the fence saying, 'Couldn't you get a proper job?' It is sometimes a good idea to start up your first business away from your home-town.

Confront your fears

Entrepreneurs don't become brave overnight. They do it little bit by little bit. They gradually confront their fears and find these fears are only powerful because they are nurtured and fed in a dark corner of their imagination.

> When I was eight, I got a part in the school play, 'Murder in the Cathedral' by T.S. Elliot. It was such a heavy piece of literature for a bunch of kids that we never got round to rehearsing the last scene - until the day of the dress rehearsal. This took place in front of every pupil in the school. The problem was – I hadn't learnt my lines. 'No problem' I thought – nor had anyone else, and someone was bound to fluff before it got to me.
>
> Except they didn't.
>
> So there I was, standing in front of 200 of my peers on stage, not having a clue what to say. The psychopathic music teacher prompted me...I still didn't know...he prompted again...silence. In front of the whole school, he walked on stage, shouted at me, hauled me off stage by my ear and cancelled the performance.
>
> So today, do I break into a cold sweat if I have present to an audience? Not at all. It was such a traumatic event that presenting to anyone at any time is a complete walk in the park compared to that.

The RAF parachute school has a great motto:

Knowledge dispels fear

To teach unsuspecting novices to jump out of a plane they practice again and again and again. They jump off benches, then off walls, then off scaffolding. By the time they get to jump out of a plane, they are so fed up with all the training, they practically throw themselves out in desperation.

You should take the same approach in business. If you are nervous about something, don't spend your whole life avoiding it. Try to find a small way to confront your fears and build up. You will find the things that most petrify you are never as bad as you'd imagined.

Some of the specific fears you might have: Throughout this book, we look at overcoming barriers and fears. However, you might be too nervous to take the plunge because of one specific fear. If so, take a look at these sections first, and how to overcome your fears, and then get into the rest of the book:

Address your fears now:

Starting a business that might fail:	*Embracing failure:* See Chapter 23
Cold calling and selling to strangers:	*How to handle rejection:* See Chapter 16
Running out of money:	*Cash is king:* See Chapter 19
Raising money:	*Inside the mind of a funder:* See Chapter 10

CHAPTER 5

Some skills that will come in very useful

Some skills that will come in very useful

You are the key to the success of your business. Your personal strengths and weaknesses will quickly become manifest in your business. However, before you subject yourself to too much grief, remember:

 No one is perfect

An artist did a project with the staff of a major company. He asked them to draw an image that best represented their chief executive. They drew a picture of a large loose cannon careering down the hill with a tiny short fuse. It made an enormous noise when it went off, but released a tiny cannon ball that only rolled three feet.

Don't beat yourself up about your weaknesses. We all have them. In fact, the most nervous public speaker I have ever heard is Richard Branson. Usually they are just the flip sides of our greatest strengths. The most important thing is that you do an honest appraisal of yourself to find what your strengths and weaknesses are so that you can compensate for them.

 Toolkit: **To help you find out what your skills and gaps are, complete the following exercise.**

Coming up with an honest assessment of yourself can be very hard to do. Try to be as honest and objective with yourself as possible. Don't be modest about your strengths, or overly critical with yourself. Think about what you enjoy doing most, and what aspects of work you don't like – these will usually correspond with your strengths and weaknesses.

If it makes it easier, rank yourself against your possible competitors, if you know them. Alternatively, ask a trusted and impartial friend to help you with this.

Strengths	
What are your advantages?	
What types of tasks do you most enjoy doing?	
What do you do well?	
What specific skills and experience do you have which might help you?	
Weaknesses	
What could you improve?	
What types of jobs do you dislike most?	
What should you avoid doing?	
Are there areas of technical knowledge or experience that you are weak in?	

Assertiveness

Being assertive is a hard thing to do well. It is not about becoming a tyrant. It is about having a deep-seated belief in your own worth.

- **Confidence:** This is the magic elixir in success. It is hard to quantify, and yet governs the economies of the world. Fundamentally, it is a belief that you have something unique to offer.

In fact, confidence is a fluid thing. It is not something we are born with, but something that gets built up over time from positive feedback we receive. It is vital you keep your self-belief constantly topped up. See Chapter 24 'Medicine for your mojo' for tips on how to do this.

- **Don't undersell yourself:** While a lack of confidence provides a very strong drive to prove yourself, it can cause you problems. You might undersell yourself, charge too low a price for your work, give in at negotiations, over-promise to your customers, or get taken for a ride by suppliers!

- **Learn to say 'no':** Success is about focus. Often you will find yourself having to politely say 'no' to potential customers or friends in order to have time left for the good stuff. It is also vital to get into the habit of telling customers when you can't do something.

> **⚑ Entrepreneur's Secret: Under-promise/over-deliver**
> If you give your client a rash promise on a delivery time and miss it by a day your client will be far more angry than if you'd told them upfront how long the job would realistically take.

I would recommend going on an assertiveness course. I know this might sound silly – I did one when I started up and a friend and I just sat giggling at the back of the class. However, it soon dawned on me that this was important stuff and it keeps cropping up throughout my life.

Time management

I love deadlines. I especially like the whooshing sound they make as they go flying by.

   Douglas Adams.

Again, doesn't time management sound a bit trivial? Well, time is the stuff life is made of.

While being busy makes you feel important, you must learn to delegate non-essential tasks

When you start out you will typically dash around doing everything from ordering stationery to scrubbing dishes. That's fine for a start (and cheap!) and gives you a good feeling for how everything works.

However, you will find that you spend only 20 per cent of your time doing the stuff that adds 80 per cent of the value to your business. Unless you work out what is essential to your business and what jobs just get in the way (or could be done better by someone else) you will be stuck doing the same thing in ten years' time. If you want to grow to a million pound business, you can't spend all day licking envelopes.

 Toolkit: **On the website there is a simple timesheet template (www.fromacorns.com). Try it with the following steps:**

- Go on a time-management course. It might cost you a few quid but it is one of the best single investments you can make. Pick up the phone now and book yourself a course. Go on, now – I mean it!
- If your work involves computers – delete all the games off your machine – NOW! Microsoft Solitaire is a sinister plot to destroy western productivity.
- Give yourself an easy task to start the day. My dad has a good theory: when he is writing he always leaves the last paragraph of his day unfinished. The next morning, he therefore has an easy way to start working again.
- Avoid interruptions – friends, the post and emails. Try to schedule a set time of day for these.
- Work out your most creative time of day. Do the most important or hard things then.
- Give yourself a break. You are not a robot – give yourself a reward once you have done your tasks. Go out for some fresh air.
- Cut yourself some slack. When planning a project, always put a

week at the end for some imaginary task. You will always need it.

- Learn to realise that just because a task is urgent, it doesn't mean it's important. By thinking and acting long term you can save a lot of crises.

The ability to listen and question

 Your aim is not to shift products. Your aim is to satisfy your customers' needs

This is the heart of selling. The most important skill is being able to find out *exactly* what your customers' needs are. The problem is that quite often they don't know themselves or won't tell you outright.

Opportunity sometimes knocks very quietly. You need to learn to be a listener, and a questioner. You also need to learn how to ask the right questions and read what your customers' hidden needs and wants might be.

For a dyed in the wool entrepreneur, this can be tricky, as you actually need to learn when to shut up!

See Chapter 16 for more information on the art of selling.

CHAPTER 6

Your winning business idea

Your winning business idea

'If you want to get rich, you need to do three things: get up early, work hard and strike oil.' (John Paul Getty, Texan oil billionaire)

 Never underestimate the importance of the right idea

It seems straightforward to have a 100 per cent annual growth rate if the industry you are in is growing by 150 per cent per year. You will be amazed at how very intelligent people have quite small businesses, or those running multinationals seem, well, not the sharpest knives in the cutlery drawer.

So spend a long time evaluating the growth potential of your idea.

If you already have an idea, it is still worth seeing if there is a spin you can put on your idea to make it more unique.

There might be a good reason no-one has thought of your "brilliant idea" before

Nine ways to come up with a good business idea

1. **It doesn't have to be your own:** It is a myth that all entrepreneurs are good at generating brilliant ideas. No – they are brilliant at making things happen. Don't be too proud to look to other people and their businesses for inspiration. If you are a natural sales person, perhaps consider teaming up with a boffin who has a cracking idea.

   One of Richard Branson's most successful businesses is his airline, but it wasn't his idea. Someone else approached him with the plans in place. Richard's genius was in making it happen.

2. **Start with what you know:** Be honest: the odds of you coming up with a new idea that people love and no one has thought of before in an industry you know nothing about are slim – to say the least. Ask a venture capitalist. They are far happier backing people who know an industry inside out, the trends, the customers, the issues, and who put a laser focus on the niche in this business that they can dominate.

3. **Don't just go for a business you 'like':** Countless people decide to run a restaurant because they like eating out, or set up a magazine because they like reading them. The quickest way to ruin a hobby is to make it your life. Instead, bear in mind that the enjoyment of running a successful business will often give you the greatest satisfaction, even if it is in an industry you wouldn't have first thought of as 'enjoyable'.

4. **Beware of 'fad' businesses:** If you can see a bandwagon, the chances are it has already left the station. Today, almost anyone can set up a web design business. If you are going to follow a trend, make sure you can offer something different. Best of all, try to spot what the next trend will be before it comes and be on the first wave.

5. **Look widely:** Cast your net widely when looking for new ideas. Look overseas for ideas, read books on the subject, read research reports on future demographic trends. Listen very closely to your customers.

6. **Look for change:** Periods of change are where lots of money can be made. This could be when there is new legislation coming to an industry, changes in customer buying habits, the opening up of an industry, or new technology.

> *New government legislation required all lorries to have covers over their loads. A young entrepreneur spotted this legislation coming up and developed a very quick-to-use and easy set of load covers.*

7. **A gap in the market, but is there a market in the gap?** It is easy to get carried away about the importance of spotting a gap in the market. A more important question is whether there is enough money in this gap.

> *A recent dot.com company cornered the market for delivering goods in 60 minutes. They had seen this done in America, and they were the first to do this in the UK. The problem was the market in the gap. They were often delivering things like aspirins and condoms worth £2 when delivery alone cost £2.50.*

8. **Competition is your friend:** A common mistake is to look for a business with no competition. There might be a very good reason why this is so. It can be much better to go to a busy business sector, but do something strikingly innovative.

9. **Put a spin on an existing business:** You don't always have to reinvent the wheel. Sometimes taking an existing business and putting a novel spin on it can ensure success.

> *Steven Greenhorn started his vehicle recovery business, 911, after a number of years of experience in the breakdown industry. His advantage lies in only employing staff who are highly qualified mechanics and can therefore fix many problems on the roadside. Steven has just opened his second depot and now employs 17 staff.*

How to come up with creative ideas

Start from a different place: Sometimes you can be too close to a business to see the obvious.

> *NASA invested millions of dollars trying to design a pen that would work properly in space where there is no gravity to push the ink down the tube.*
>
> *The Russians used a pencil.*

Our brains are fundamentally lazy and will continually try to make the obvious conclusions. The trick is to try to surprise your brain into doing something new.

> *'There is nothing that is a more certain sign of insanity than to do the same thing over and over and expect the results to be different.' (Albert Einstein)*

Here are some ways to do this:

- Start by thinking of opposites – think of the worst things you could do for your customer.
- Try to think of funny ideas – this is sometimes the brain's way of disguising genuinely exciting opportunities.
- Change your routine. Deliberately take a different route to work, and look around. I get my best ideas when I have a hangover and jot them into a special 'hangover book'.
- Start with your customer

Don't knock it. Hangovers can be a great source of business ideas

Share your ideas: Remember the kids in school exams who would put their arms round their papers so no one would copy them? Don't become like them. For sure, don't go and tell your nearest competitors all your creative ideas, but by the same token, don't try to hoard and lock up your best ideas – this will stifle your creativity completely. Remember success is more about perspiration and timing than just a simple idea.

You have to be careful about who you brainstorm with. Sometimes it can be easier with relative strangers who will have no preconceptions and won't judge you. Whoever you do it with, it is important to have this vital rule:

Don't judge the results: The aim is to shut down the critical faculties of your brain, to allow all the creative bits to come to the fore. If you start laughing or mocking others, this part of your brain will clam up instantly. The idea is to do a 'creative dump' – put all the ideas down on the table and make sure no one makes any comment about how good the ideas are.

Think laterally: Look at other countries for ideas. Some of the best businesses have been imported from other countries. Similarly, you could import ideas from another sector or industry.

> *Richard Davies was working as a fishing ghillie in Stornoway when a friend back from the States gave him some beef jerky to taste. Richard was hooked. It was very tasty, it was very healthy with only around 3 per cent fat, up to a whopping 50 per cent protein and only 64 calories per serving. When he did some homework he found in the States it was a $1 billion market.*
>
> *However, it was not possible to import US jerky into the EU because of stringent laws about US beef. At first Richard tried to make his own, but found no one would teach him. However, in the process he came across King B, a South American jerky supplier. He now imports this into UK, and sells under the name Wild West Jerky (**www.wildwest-jerky.co.uk**). Sales are growing exponentially for Richard, and he has won a medal from the Guild of Fine Food Retailers.*

CHAPTER 7

Turning your ideas into a business plan

Turning your ideas into a business plan

If you don't know where you are going, it doesn't matter which road you take to get there. (Alice's Adventures in Wonderland)

One of your first tasks will be to write a business plan. There are hundreds of books, training courses, software programs, websites and guides devoted to them.

Before throwing yourself headlong into this process, there are three basic rules you should apply.

Three rules of business plans

1. Think of your audience: The most important audience for your plan is yourself. This is the one opportunity where you think through all the implications of your business, and really check the assumptions you are making. For this reason, there is no simple template you must follow. It is also vital that this is your plan. There is no point paying an accountant to write the plan for you when you are going to be running the business.

The second most important audience is a potential funder. At this stage, your plan becomes a sales tool to raise you the finance.

2. Avoid paralysis by analysis: It is easy to spend too long on a plan and get bogged down in the detail. I remember seeing a business plan for a café where they had worked the costs out down to the last teaspoon.

I think it is underpinned by a psychological desire to make business seem like a predictable science, rather than the inexact human endeavour it actually is.

As a rule of thumb, when you find yourself classifying headlines with different colour codes – step away from the plan. Instead, let your mantra be that of Texan billionaire Ross Perot:

'When I see a snake – I kill it. I don't appoint a committee on snakes.'

3. Keep planning: As von Clausewitz, a Prussian general, said:

No plan survives the first contact with the enemy*

*(or your customers in this case).

Almost as soon as your plan is written, it will be out of date. However, the most successful businesses are those that are continually adapting to changes in customers and the market. It is vital that your plan, once written, isn't consigned to the bottom drawer or the file marked 'dustbin'. Look at Chapter 18 for advice on strategy.

Where too many business plans are filed

What will a potential funder look for in your plan?

Most people produce a business plan mainly to raise money. I have sat on many funding panels, and spoken to many bank managers, and it is useful to bear in mind the thoughts that might go through the mind of a funder when you go to see them.

Typically, in a one hour meeting, they will go through the following progression:

Do I think *you* have what it takes to make this work (usually decided within 120 seconds of you walking through the front door)?

Does the overall business concept excite me (four minutes)?

Can you reassure me that I will ever see my money again (the remaining 40 minutes or so)?

OK, so the clock is running: let's address them in order:

00:00

01:20

You: Whether you are asking for £5, £5,000 or £500,000, the following is always true:

Investors back people

No matter what your idea, funders are ultimately betting on your ability to make things happen. So how can you prove this?

- It's unfair, but first impressions *do* count. An experienced interviewer from a leading company once told me she usually decided on a candidate 40 seconds after they had walked in the door! So, look after the simple things. Dress smart, look people in the eye when you walk in, smile and shake hands. It makes a difference.

- Put details of any relevant experience in your plan. This could be work experience in your industry, or better, examples of previous businesses you have run, or examples of your own initiative (you organised a fashion show at school? Put it in).

- Put in an analysis of your strengths and weaknesses. Don't make out you are superhuman, what they are looking for is an honest appreciation of your strengths and what you will do to balance your weaknesses.

- The most important thing is gumption, or staying power. Success will ultimately depend on your ability to keep going through tough times. Try to put examples of your drive and determination in your plan. Funders will also want to know you have thought things through. Be prepared to answer a whole range of 'what if' questions from your funders.

05:20

Excite me: This is where you get people hooked with your sexy idea. The secret here is to keep it simple; outline the concept, summarise the main points. It should briefly look at your competitive position and, this is the clincher, why *your idea is different.* It is going to be hard to excite someone about backing another window cleaning business, but what's this? You are a former climber, and are the only person in Leeds who specialises in tall office buildings? Now I'm interested. Now all you have to do is...

60:00

Reassure me: This is where we get to making sure your figures stack up. On to the next chapter!

CHAPTER 8

Forecasting your financial future

Forecasting your financial future

If you look at any business plan books you are likely to be daunted by the financials you are required to produce: balance sheets, P&L, three year discounted cashflow, return on capital invested, binomial quadratic distribution, warp drive integer derivative...

Let's stick to the basics.

Your revenue

This is the total amount of cash you receive. This typically depends on two things; the price you sell things for, and the number you can sell (I told you we were going to keep it basic).

Price

Price should not be determined by the cost of your product. Your price is what your customers are willing to pay and, as you might have seen with things like iced-mocha-cappuccinos, this can bear little relation to the cost. Price is a marketing issue – look at Chapter 14. However, you have to know your break-even price – the *minimum* price you have to charge for each item to cover costs. We come on to this in a moment.

The number you sell

This is determined by two things, how big the market is and how many you can physically make and sell in a day. To determine the size of the market, you need to do some market research. This needs looking at in detail as getting this wrong can have a serious impact on your business.

How to forecast your sales

> **Use research like a drunk uses a lamp-post –**
> **more for support than illumination**

Accurate market research is a notoriously tricky business – just look at election forecasts.

The dot.com boom and bust era was largely based on faulty market research, and much of it still goes on. This is what I call:

Waynestock Syndrome

> *In Wayne's World 2, they are planning to hold a rock concert*
> *– Waynestock. They are worried about how many people*
> *will come until Jim Morrison appears in Wayne's dream and*
> *says: 'Hold it, and they will come.'*

To follow this dot.com approach for your business, do a variation on the following:

1. You are selling Amazonian fighting fish. You do some research on the internet to find the total size of your likely customer group. This could be, say, the total number of houses with ponds in the Manchester area, or the number of people in the UK last year who bought goldfish.

2. Make a modest assumption that, say, 1 per cent of this market should be yours in the first year, going up to 5 per cent, then 10 per cent in the following years. This will give you a first year revenue, or turnover, of £300,000. Sounds good!

3. ...er, that's it.

The problem with this approach, as you will have doubtless spotted, is that while the figures will seem modest, you have absolutely *no evidence* that people will buy one fish from you, let alone 10,000 of them.

This is the problem with making assumptions.

> *If you ASSUME you make an ASS of U and ME.*
>
> *(Silence of the Lambs)*

The only reliable way to make assumptions is to base them on experience.

In an ideal world, you will have already tried selling some products before doing your business plan. By analysing these sales (how long did it take to get each customer? do they fit in a distinct category like 'retired hobbyists'? did they just buy from you because they were friends?), you can then realistically extend your forecasts.

Alternatively, you might have worked for an employer in this industry. Their figures should give you some indication. Again, make sure there are no underlying things you are missing out – i.e. it took then six years to build up to their current customer base, or their biggest customer also happens to be a relative (I know one large company where this was the case).

You might have a wise mentor who has been and done this all before and can tell you just what to do (see Chapter 18 about hunting and capturing one of these mythical beasts).

Find out how your competitors are doing. You can apply various covert techniques, but by far the most effective I have found is just to phone them up and ask them point blank. You'll be amazed at how much they will tell you. People love to brag about themselves, and will often not see humble little you as a competitor. Again, put these figures through a reality filter. Are they deliberately under-estimating to put you off? Does the bulk of their sales come from one customer they are not going to tell you about? Perhaps try to verify these stories from their staff or competitors.

You can also do your own research. This is not always as accurate as you might think.

> Before producing my first university yearbook, I did a survey into what students would want to see in it, the ideal price, and whether they would buy one. I then produced the book on these assumptions. However, I discovered that telling someone you will pay £10 is very different from actually having to hand over £10 that could be spent on beer. I also found the real customers were their parents, and they would pay double that.

Beware of just researching among friends. If someone (particularly a friend) asked what you thought of their lovingly crafted porcelain angels, would you (a) be callous, point out what dross they are and they should never give up the day job, or (b) smile sweetly, nod and back gently away…?

Entrepreneur's Secret: Funders love 'letters of intent'
Providing a sheaf of letters confirming that 'Dear Mr Smith, I will definitely be ordering ten Amazonian fighting fish the moment they clear customs' is very impressive (but don't think they won't notice if they all have suspiciously similar handwriting...).

Your costs

Having worked out your revenue, you then need to calculate costs. There are two types of cost:

1. Your direct costs
2. Your overhead costs

1. Direct costs

This is the cost of producing each item. It is made up of two elements:

Raw material cost: This is the cost of the 'ingredients' in each product. Some of these will be obvious, but also look at hidden costs. If you are making pottery, don't just put in the cost of the clay; also estimate an element of the electricity or gas used to fire the item.

The cost of your time: One of the biggest oversights people make starting out in business is failing to:

> **Make sure you cost your own time properly**

I'll illustrate. You want to sell your product for £5. The raw materials cost about 60p, but it takes you about two hours to produce, pack and deliver each item. You don't care because you are keen and eager. Orders take off. Soon, you are working flat out 60 hours a week producing your goods, but you are stuck. You could employ someone else to do the work, but their hourly rate will be £4.50. Even by getting production time down to one hour, you are making a loss of 10p each hour this person works with you.

Of course, your £5 might be a market-entry pricing strategy to get market share before whacking your price up. If so, see the notes in Chapter 14 about increasing your price.

This all sounds obvious I know, but many people fall into this trap. Be careful to include:

- How much time realistically goes into each item. Include time to purchase your supplies, set-up time, packing and delivery time, how long it takes to invoice for each item, and then chase payment.
- Put in an honest rate for how much you would have to pay *someone else* to do your job. If yours is a specialist skill, or requires a unique blend of persuasive personality, don't assume you can get someone for £4.50 an hour to replace you.

> 🐜 **Entrepreneur's Secret for service businesses: How many can you sell?**
>
> If you are a running a service business, you will be selling your own time. As an energetic entrepreneur, you will probably put the number of hours in the day as your work time. This is a mistake. You need to include travel time between jobs, seasonal fluctuations, holidays, customers missing appointments, time off to do your sales and book-keeping. A more realistic capacity is probably around 65 per cent. This also applies if you take on other members of staff.

2. Overhead costs

On top of the cost for producing each item, you will also have fixed or overhead costs that you will incur no matter how hard you work. Examples include rent for your premises, marketing costs, telephone, professional fees, car loans etc.

As the name implies, these costs will hang over your head regardless of how many fighting fish you sell. There will often be a few days of the week or months of the year where business will be slow. But your overhead costs won't go away. Therefore, it stands to reason you want to:

 Keep your overheads as low as possible

Turn to Chapter 9 on 'Bootstrapping' for some advice on how to do this.

One of your most important overhead costs is you. Don't do what I did when I started out and forget to include your own salary and just take it from profits. The risk here is that there will often be no profits, and when there are, the temptation is to take them all out and buy yourself a shiny new TV.

First, work out your minimum survival budget.

Then set this as a salary that comes out by standing order from your bank account. Get into the discipline of only increasing this when you know you can sustain it for at least four months. If you want a greater incentive, then pay yourself a sales bonus for each new piece of work you bring in.

Break-even point

Once you know how many you *could* sell, you need to work out how many you *must* sell to meet your overhead costs.

As well as a break-even price, there is also a break-even level of sales. As some of your costs are fixed overheads (in particular, the amount you need to live on), there is a minimum number of items you must sell in a year to cover your fixed costs. When you calculate your projections, make sure this level at least covers your overheads.

Business plan checklist

Now that you've thought about why and for whom you're producing your plan, you should be ready to put one together. Overleaf is a simple checklist, or you can get similar forms from banks or enterprise agencies. But remember – this is your plan, not theirs!

What should go in your plan:

Brief summary of your idea

- What the market is, and why your idea is unique. Forecasted profits. Longer term prospects. How much finance is required.

You and your team

- Track record with key achievements for yourself.
- Other people who will be helping you.
- An honest appreciation of your strengths and weaknesses, and what you will do to bridge these.

Your product or service

- A brief description of what it is and what needs it is servicing.
- Your target market (current size and your predictions on growth). Put the main points here and keep any detailed supporting statistics to the appendix.
- A more detailed analysis of the specific niche your product/service will fit.
- Your competitors: who are the prime ones and how will you compete against them?
- What are the unique selling points of your product/service?
- A SWOT analysis: your strengths, weaknesses, opportunities and threats.

Sales and marketing

- Your price, and how you decided on this.
- Place: where will you be selling your product from.
- Who will do the selling.
- What promotional plans you have.

Operations management

- Suppliers.
- Equipment needed.

Financials

- Your forecasts, and the EVIDENCE behind your assumptions.
- Monthly cashflow forecast for year one, and quarterly for year two.
- Profit and loss forecast.
- Balance sheet.

CHAPTER 9

Low-risk ways to start in business

Low-risk ways to start in business

You have your idea and are ready to take the plunge. Now is a time to take a piece of wisdom from the mountaineer Chris Bonnington, or to be more precise – his mum:

> ### Do dangerous things safely

It's a great principle. Any muppet can pack in their job, re-mortgage their house and leap into a business without thought. It takes a much more canny operator to work hard to minimise all the risks before they start. This should become your mantra in every business endeavour.

There are some ways to do this when you start up.

Some lower-risk start-up strategies

Get your existing employer to support you: A brilliant way to start is to have your current employer as your main customer. This is not as ludicrous as it may sound, and many entrepreneurs have started up this way. You might be taking away an unprofitable part of their business that they are happy to see the back of, or you might become a great supplier for them.

Corporate venturing/intrapreneurship: An alternative is to start up your business within the auspices of a large company. On one hand, you might have to accept a lower level of ownership of the business, and have to take on board a wider range of viewpoints when making your decision. On the plus point, they will support you through the critical start-up phase, give you access to a wide range of resources and hopefully provide your initial customers or leads. And at the end of the day, you might prefer 25 per cent of a £1m company rather than 100 per cent of one which struggles to turn over £100,000.

There are variations on this such as trying to fit your start-up in around the hours of your current day job. This might be a good chance for you to do your homework. However, beyond this, your day job and your start-up are likely to suffer. Also don't be tempted to try and poach your employer's customers. This is generally illegal, not to say unethical, and an employer can slap an injunction on you pretty quickly. Far better to go with their blessing.

Get another source income: This could be a part-time job, though this can cause a problem of a lack of focus and commitment to your main business. If you are very lucky, you might have a partner with a regular income to support you.

Franchising

Franching is simply using somebody else's system for running a business. This used to be looked down on, but there is absolutely no reason to be sniffy – there are over 30,000 franchised outlets in the UK and over 93 per cent claim to be profitable.

The benefits are that you are getting a tried and tested concept, and a proven brand so you can hit the ground running and should have a more rapid build of turnover.

You also get support, training and the chance to share best practice around a network.

Of course, this comes at a price. You will usually have to pay something like an initial franchise fee, a management services fee or royalty, an advertising levy and/or product mark-up.

And this cost is not just financial. Running a franchise is more restrictive – the franchisor will have systems you will be expected to adhere to, performance levels you will have to meet, and they will be able to inspect you.

Generally speaking, if your primary concern in running a business is to earn a good regular income then this is something you should look at seriously. If on the other hand you want a high degree of personal freedom and control then perhaps it is not for you.

Visit the British Franchise Association website **www.british-franchise.org** for an excellent range of information into all things franchising.

Of course, one of the lowest risk ways is not to take a financial risk. That brings us to bootstrapping.

The beauty of bootstrapping

Bootstrapping is an American term. It means starting out with no money. Many large companies like Microsoft originally started up with just pennies. There is a lot to be said for bootstrapping the start of your business.

For a start, you can make mistakes on the cheap. You will never get it right first time and without large debts you can change tack mid-stream.

You don't know what your customers want until you actually start selling it to them. For example, you might have decided to open a retail outlet, only to find your customers are happier buying from you over the phone.

Give yourself time to deal with the Law of Unintended Consequences (see page 111). In other words, give yourself financial space to find out what customers really want from you.

And besides, surviving with little money gives you a good financial discipline as you grow.

Some bootstrapping techniques

Get your customers to pay for your set up: This might sound a little strange, but don't overlook your customers as a source of start-up finance. If you are developing a product that will lead to real cost savings or benefits for a client, and that doesn't exist somewhere else, see if the client will help fund the development by paying a deposit for the order.

A designer produced a prototype version of a novel Christmas decoration. He took it to a major retailer who loved it, and ordered 10,000. He then offered them a 10 per cent discount if they would pay a deposit upfront for the order, which they were happy to do. He used this to pay for his manufacturing.

Ask yourself, do you really need it? The best approach is to spend as little as possible. Think through every purchase you want to make and ask if it is essential. Do you have to have a brand new shiny computer/car, or can this wait? Do you need an office, or can you start off working from home (see the next section). Can you 'incubate' your business in the offices of a larger company? You will find many of your proposed outgoings are things you want rather than need for your start-up.

Don't buy outright: If you really need a major capital expenditure, see if you can rent, lease or borrow it rather than buy it outright. The temptation when you start out is to think you need to own all your equipment in order to function, but this just isn't true. By leasing your major purchases, you can update to better equipment quickly and cheaply when the money rolls in, or change quickly if your market is not where you thought it was.

Negotiate and shop around: Everything is negotiable. Always ask for a discount when you buy things. Ask if there is a discount for paying in cash, or paying early. The worst thing they can say is no.

Get good prices from your suppliers: People get so carried away in squeezing a few extra pennies from customers, they forget that saving money from your suppliers can have a huge impact on profitability.

Get them to do some creative thinking. Tell them what your budget is, and what your end product will do. Then ask them if they can think of any creative ways to deliver this.

Don't get lazy and stick with the status quo. Make sure that you shop around at least once a year to see if you can get better prices. At the very least, it will keep your current suppliers on their toes. Think about it – you know how much harder you'd work if your customers were regularly shopping around.

When negotiating with suppliers, you could borrow the 'daft lassie' technique:

A young woman built up a very successful retail jewellery business, starting from a market stall in Glasgow's Barrowland market. When negotiating with suppliers, and particularly professionals, she said she perfected the art of

asking 'daft lassie' questions such as 'Instead of paying you
an upfront fee, why don't you take a commission on what
you save me?' The suppliers were amazed that no one had
asked them before, and, as often as not, said yes.

Working from home vs. an office

When starting out, consider working from home. It's not ideal, but
if you have a couple of lean months you will not have to worry
about rent and other associated costs.

David Jones set up his computer company, DMA Design,
from his bedroom while still a computer science student.
His first two games provided enough royalties to keep him
going while he developed his third. This was Lemmings,
and it sold 60,000 copies within a few days and went on to
become a worldwide best-seller.

What is important is that you keep a separation between your
home and work life. If possible, have one room that is exclusively
used for work. Another tip from an entrepreneur is to consider
'commuting' to your home. Before you start work, at lunch time,
and at the end of the day – get out of your house and go for a walk.
This can be a great way to separate your two lives.

If you are taking on an office or premises, don't automatically go
for expensive city-centre locations. Unless you are a retail business,
in most instances you will have to visit your clients and not the
other way round.

> **♟ Entrepreneur's Secret:**
> Be VERY wary of signing long leases – you will not be able to
> escape these even if your business stops.

Of course, working from home can be a little difficult if you are
taking on staff:

I remember interviewing for an early member of staff when
I worked from home. I had done everything I could to
disguise the fact that my bed was in the corner of the room.
The whole way through the interview I had to repeat a

mantra to myself, 'Don't glance at the bed, don't glance at the bed...'

Starting up in partnership with someone

Many people are tempted to start up in partnership with someone to help reduce the risks. In an ideal world, this is because they have complementary skills. However, more commonly it is because they are afraid of doing it on their own.

Bear in mind: the German for partnership is 'Partnershaft'. I have seen businesses torn apart by warring partners. The problem is that a small business can place great pressures on people, and over time partners can grow apart. It's like marrying the first person you go out with. Try the following litmus test:

1. Be honest with yourself, are you just doing this because you are nervous? Don't apologise for this, if you are not pretty wound-up going into business, you certainly ought to be. It's just that there are much easier ways of building up a support network that will give you everything a partner would (see page 151).

2. If you are doing it for strategic reasons, for instance you have different skills you could not find elsewhere, then draw up a detailed partnership agreement at the outset. This should cover exactly what the two (or more) of you are going to be specifically responsible for, and what you'll do if you change your minds in future. I know this feels a bit like drawing up a pre-nuptial agreement, but you can then file it in a bottom drawer and (hopefully) never look at it again.

There is an exception to this:

Going into partnership with your wife, husband or lover

This so goes against all rational business logic that it can often work extremely well in practice. I have seen many husband and wife partnerships that result in very fulfilling personal and business lives. Maybe it's because you've made such a commitment you have no option but to succeed?

Still, there are some things you can do to make this easier:

- Be as professional as possible: treat each other as employees. Have clear job descriptions about where your roles and responsibilities begin and end. This extends to how you communicate with each other – you wouldn't call a member of staff 'a lazy good for nothing waste of space' (hopefully), so resist the temptation to do this to your partner.
- If you have staff, include them in communication. Bear in mind that for them it can feel as if there is a secret society which operates around the kitchen sink where all the real decisions are made. Try to keep to formal lines of reporting, and have regular meetings.
- Keep work at work. Try to come up with a strict line in your house past which business doesn't go. This could be a threshold in the house, or a time at night. Otherwise your work worries will follow you everywhere and things will get very old very quickly.

CHAPTER 10

Raising finance

Raising finance

Sometimes bootstrapping your birth would just compromise the development of your idea, so you have to spend money to make money. The following are the most obvious sources of finance:

Sources of finance

Your own savings: There is nothing like spending your own hard earned dosh to really focus your mind. It is also a great sign to other investors, who are much more likely to come in if they can see you are taking an equal personal risk.

At the same time, keep some savings. It is a timeless rule of business that you will need more money than you anticipated. It also makes it much easier to sleep at night knowing you have a little emergency cash stashed away.

> ♟ **Entrepreneur's Secret:** Regularly put some savings into a 30-day notice account. They pay a little more interest but, more importantly, the notice period stops you from taking money out when you don't need to.

Tax rebate: If you have been paying tax for a few years, you might be able to claim a rebate on this if you don't make a profit in your first year, thus releasing some finance.

From family and friends: You may think this is the cheapest source of money, and in real terms it often can be. However, the emotional cost of this can be huge. If you are going to borrow from friends and family – do it professionally. Draw up a simple agreement that says what they are getting for this investment and what the intended repayment schedule will be.

> ### ♟ Entrepreneur's Secret: Credit cards
> There are many stories of ballsy American entrepreneurs who borrow lots of money on credit cards and use this to start up. OK, it might be easy, but it is both incredibly risky and incredibly expensive. The risk is that you get stuck in a spiral of debt, using one card to pay off another and all the time facing interest rates of up to 20 per cent. You don't need that kind of stress!

Venture capitalists: There is probably more hot air expended on this topic than anything else in small business. Whatever the merits or otherwise of VCs, it is very unlikely you will get one to invest in your start-up venture. They have increasingly high investment thresholds and are looking for relatively short-term exit for their investment. Far more interesting are:

Business angels: Like a VC, an angel will typically expect equity in the business, but there the similarities end. A business angel is normally a wealthy individual (or sometimes a consortium of individuals) who is investing for the longer term in the business. Their interest is usually more personal in the business, and they will get a range of tax breaks for their investment. They should also be able to bring skills or contacts with them and a willingness to get involved with the nitty gritty of the business. This can sometimes be as much value as their cash, earning them the term 'sweat equity'. There are formal angel networks you can approach (see the appendix: Useful sources of information). Alternatively, you might know a wealthy individual who has perhaps made a capital gain recently and might be interested.

In business, angels do exist

From the bank: Sooner or later, you will end up at the bank, either to deposit your well-gotten gains, or cap in hand to borrow money.

Many people are nervous about going to banks. The secret is to think of them as a 'money shop' – they want to 'sell' money to good prospects – they only make a profit from the money they lend out and make interest on.

How to get a bank to lend you money

The first stage is to reassure them you are a good bet (look at Chapter 7 on the business plan). Present them with a professional image. Show them you have done your homework and take this seriously. It will also reassure them if you have a range of finance from different sources: your savings, other sponsors and orders from customers.

Secondly, shop around. As with anything else you are 'buying', it pays to shop around. If you don't get an offer, or you don't like the one you've got – don't worry. There are plenty more sources of cash, and it will only cost you a bit of boot leather.

> *They give me an umbrella when it's dry and demand it back when it rains*

This is a consistent gripe against banks. During the last recession, there was a element of truth to this as many banks had made some bad lending decisions. However, since then they've tightened up their act. Anyway, they are businesses too and not charities. It's up to you to make sure this doesn't happen to you.

Ask early

If a friend came to you in desperation begging for urgent cash for their business, while sympathetic, wouldn't you be a little nervous about lending it to them? The trick is always to ask for more money than you might need, and ask for it early on. The bank will be far more impressed with your cautious approach, and your long-term planning.

Keep in touch

As with any customer or supplier, it is vital to keep a good relationship. When you win new work, tell your bank, or send them press cuttings. They are more likely to lend to someone they know, like and trust.

The Prince's Trust

If you are under 30 (or 26 in Scotland), the Prince's Trust and the Prince's Scottish Youth Business Trust, are a fantastic source of support and finance when starting out in business. I got my start-up from them and have been a strong supporter ever since.

Their position is 'the lender of last resort' – they are there to lend money when you have exhausted all other sources. Of course, they give you far more than the money, and it is almost worth borrowing money from them just to get access to all of their services. You might also find other banks are willing to lend to you once the Trust is on board as they respect their lending decisions.

> 'PSYBT gave me the support and finance I needed to start my business, when others would not help. Now as a Board Member, I have a fantastic opportunity to help young people.' (Michelle Mone, founder of the Ultimo bra).

Government support

The government's role is to step in where there is a gap in market provision.

Small Firms Loan Guarantee Scheme

This is one of the most popular support schemes. In the case of the SFLGS, the government recognises some businesses will not be able to provide security for their borrowing. Under this scheme, if you can show that you have been refused funding because of a lack of security, the DTI can step in and guarantee 75 per cent of the loan, in return for a premium you pay them on the loan. You can apply for this scheme through your bank, who will guide you through the required stages.

Grants and other support

The government has a wide range of other schemes and assistance packages. There are two tips here:

Don't get too hung-up on trying to get 'free' money. Grants are the holy grail of start-ups, and it is a myth to think there are large amounts of free money swilling around. You will also have to be very professional about how you apply for this money, and the process can often be very lengthy.

There is much more that the government can support you with other than cash. For example, there are training courses, e-commerce schemes, help in employing people, assistance in exploring new export markets or innovation. Tap into this network as soon as you start your business plans through your Business Link in England or Local Enterprise Company in Scotland (see the appendix: Useful sources of information).

CHAPTER 11

The dreaded legals

The dreaded legals

Most business start-up guides have acres of information on legal issues. Being all legalled-up to the nines will not make you a business success. However, ignoring the most basic legal issues can quickly put you under.

There is a variety of red tape you have to be aware of when you start up. There is an excellent government guide that gives an overview of the tax and legal issues for start-ups. You can get it from **www.inlandrevenue.gov.uk/startingup/index.htm** or by calling 08459 15 45 15.

It is also likely you will require the use of a lawyer. The rule of thumb here is:

 Treat lawyers like prophylactics (i.e. condoms)

Lawyers are there to prevent problems from happening. I would advise you to see one now so that you don't have to see one later. Spending a bit of time at the outset can save you a huge amount of grief later. Also, like your prophylactics, don't just go for the cheapest – it can be tricky to get a refund if things go wrong later...

> *For refund, insert baby. (Sign on condom vending machine in London underground)*

Get a legal MOT

Ask your lawyer to do an MOT for you. My lawyers did this for me, and it was excellent value. It should take a maximum of two hours where they run through all the main risks and legal issues that you should be aware of, from the right legal form for your business to contracts, insurance, copyright and so on. At the end of this, you should have a checklist.

Don't panic!

You don't have to deal with all of these immediately. Business is all about taking calculated risks, you just have to prioritise which ones you can deal with, and afford.

If a lawyer is not prepared to do this, then you should question whether they just want to get the maximum fees out of you.

Don't worry, you can't protect yourself from *every* risk

Avoid legal action wherever possible

A good lawyer will be the first to tell you this – if a dispute ends up in court, then everyone loses. Most legal disputes seem to arise from two common causes, which you should avoid:

1. Poor communication: For example, agreeing a contract with a customer is just a process of talking through all the possible eventualities so there can be no misunderstanding in the future.

2. Ego: Many people take court action because they feel aggrieved and bruised. Sure, you feel wronged, and it is like a slap in the face. But is it really worth it *for the business* to spend thousands of pounds and months of time taking someone to court. The risk is, you win the battle but lose the war.

> *A small software company found Microsoft had inadvertently copied one of their designs. Feeling aggrieved, they took the giant to court, and after a protracted battle, won their case. The company went bust shortly afterwards.*

Should I be a limited company?

When you start in business, you can take two basic legal forms:

Sole trader (or partnership): This is the simplest form. It requires little or no paperwork, and is simplest from a tax point of view. A downside is that the business is you – there is no other distinct legal entity to protect you. Should you go bust, people can come after you personally for any debts you have.

It often makes sense to start as a sole trader or partnership (two or more people), but there's no reason why you shouldn't stay as one if you wish. John Lewis, the department store chain, is still a partnership.

Limited company: A limited company is a distinct legal entity separate from you, the individual (even if you own all the shares). You become an employee of the business, and are not automatically chased for all the debts if things go wrong. If, like me when I first realised this, you are thinking 'Why would anyone in their right minds *not* want to limit their liability?', then bear the following in mind.

Given that you have a degree of protection, there comes an equivalent responsibility. You have to file your accounts at Companies House (which means your competitors can look at them), and beyond a certain turnover level, they have to be audited. Also, as a director, there are certain standards you have to comply with (such as not continuing to trade when you know you are insolvent). Failure to comply can result in legal action.

There is also a very different tax regime as a company. Now you are taxed both on your salary (as any paid employee is) and, in addition, on the profits your business makes.

Finally, funders are obviously wise to the benefits of incorporation. They will therefore often expect you to give personal guarantees on any of your borrowings. So if your business loan is secured against your house – what limits on your liability do you *really* have?

There is no simple answer. You must speak to an accountant who can guide you through what is right for your personal circumstances and stage of business (see page 124).

CHAPTER 12

Guerrilla marketing

Guerrilla marketing

Definition: 'Marketing on a tight budget'. (Not to be confused with Gorilla Marketing)

A hungry entrepreneur will be tempted to skip this section and go straight out selling. Before you do, consider:

> **The cleverer you are with your marketing, the easier your sales will be**

A quick definition

Marketing covers everything required to get your product or service to meet a customer's need. It is taught as the 4 Ps:

- Your product (or service)
- The place you sell it from
- Your price
- Finally, promotion, or how you get your customers.
  Let's look at each in turn:

Your product or service

You may think you know what product or service you are going to offer, but just consider the following few points:

> **A customer is not interested in your product/service – they are interested in what it can do for them**

Forget features – sell the benefits

If this sounds obvious, then wonder, why are computers always sold just on the size of their hard-drive and whizzy technical specifications? Look at Apple Computers who, when they launched their iMac computers, had the genius to make them visually stunning, and bring them out in a range of 'flavours' (and the lime-flavoured version sold out).

When you get too close to your product, it is easy to forget what the actual benefits are to your customers. The following exercise should help you around this:

Toolkit: The Acme Benefit Generator

Make a list of five *features* of your product or your service in the first column. In the second column, add in the benefit of each feature to your client. These benefits are how you should describe and market your business.

Feature	Benefit
Example: *I use a stronger wood to make my furniture*	Which means for the customer: *Furniture built to last you a lifetime*
1.	
2.	
3.	
4.	
5.	

Once you have a list of benefits, these and not the features should form the basis of your marketing.

Understand what business you are in

I know this sounds stupid, but consider:

> *Parker Pens revolutionised their business when they realised they were not a pen company but a gift company. Customers tended to buy their pens as presents, and in that case their nearest competition was not other pens but golf clubs, wallets and carriage clocks.*

This is an extension of the last exercise, but you have to ask yourself continually what people are *really* buying from you.

> *Jennifer thinks people will come to her café because it's cheap. But perhaps they just want a break from the office at lunchtime. In that case, why not put out a plentiful supply of newspapers and comfy chairs? Or perhaps they are just very pushed for time? In which case, why not offer to deliver the food to their office? And while you're at it, why not offer them pre-cooked fresh food they can heat up for their supper?*

What do people really want from your gardening service: just someone else to do the back-breaking labour, or is it botanical knowledge, or creative flair? Depending on which, you could offer a service for other labour-intensive jobs, or a free design consultation, or a regular mailer on which plants are in season.

Don't just be blinkered by what customers have bought in the past, or what your competition is doing – think what they *might* want but no one has thought to offer them.

Be different

You can gain a great advantage over your competitors not by spending huge amounts on marketing, but just by being different from everyone else. The more unique the selling point of your product, the easier it is going to be for you to sell. Of course, this has to be an advantage that offers real value to your customers. If your only advantage is a cheaper price, it is going to be a long hard slog for you.

You can be different in any number of ways. It could be the way your product is delivered:

Peter Wood became a multimillionaire and revolutionised the centuries-old insurance industry. How? He just used a bright red telephone. But before Direct Line, no one else had thought of selling insurance direct to customers over the phone.

It could be an extra added feature of your product that no one else offers:

A carpet fitting company offered computer-aided design for hotels. Previously, to fit new carpets, a hotel would have to shut for days just to do the measuring. With the new service, this could all be planned in advance by computer, resulting in only half the closure time. This had huge benefits for customers.

It can be the way your product is packaged:

When Belinda Jarron set up her business supplying plants and flowers for offices, she decided to call it Fleurtations. She painted her vans bright pink and gave her staff colourful outfits. One of her main competitors is 'Rentokil', so it is easy to see how this might be an advantage.

Probably my favourite entrepreneur is a Scots-Italian called Gio Benedetti. He has made 'difference' his mantra, and made a lot of money along the way.

His latest business is a redesign of the humble first-aid box. The traditional green box hasn't been redesigned for decades. Gio has launched a new one. It is based on the shape of his Porsche; the smooth opening device is modelled on the ashtray of his Jaguar (see what I mean about the entrepreneur bit). There is a thermometer strip on the outside, and lots of easy tape dispensers. Sure it costs a bit more than the old one, but it is so much easier to use, and is now sold in stores around the UK.

Your brand

You've got your product/service – now you have to give it a brand. Most of you will now think – 'Hmm, branding sounds like a big expensive word for a small business, maybe I'll skip this section.' Stick with me on this one.

Take a couple of moments now to think back to the last major purchase you made. I bet at the time there was a real feeling of excitement? I would also wager that by about now, there is also a considerable degree of fear; have I bought the right one, will it break down, could I have bought it cheaper?

Buying stuff is scary. Over many years of selling, and listening to others, I have come to the following, rather cynical conclusion:

People often don't want the best – they want the least worst

The number of times I've heard of someone who lost work when the client said 'You were the best proposal, but we went with someone who was bigger'. It makes me want to scream and start to gnaw my leather restraining straps.

This is what a brand is – it is about trust. In a confusing and increasingly busy world, customers want to plump for what they feel safest with. It's your job to reassure them.

Large companies spend millions on branding. Many small companies do it far better with almost zilch.

Branding on a tight budget

Before you come over all corporate and logo-tastic, bear in mind the following:

Your business has one huge branding advantage – you: Don't always apologise for being small. Customers often like the fact that it's your raggedy butt on the line if things go wrong. They know where you live and can phone you up at 3am and demand delivery. This counts for a lot. So don't always hide behind an anonymous 'corporate' identity. Bring more of yourself into the brand.

Alistair Rutherford built up Edinburgh Preserves selling home-made chutneys. After a few years of hard graft they started getting orders from the big supermarkets. Al decided it was time to become a bit more professional. He brought in a design agency to produce new labels and packaging. When he showed these to the supermarket buyer, they were horrified and made him dump them. The reason his

products sold so well was precisely because they didn't look
professional and mass-produced!

Be original: We are being swamped with marketing:

- It is estimated that the average consumer sees about one million marketing messages a year.
- Last year in America $100 billion was spent on direct marketing. A 1 per cent response rate is good – 2 per cent will usually get a marketer a promotion.
- Google currently searches over 3 billion websites.
- A typical modern household has access to 32 TV channels.

To cut through this noise, you need original thinking.

A couple of years ago we launched an e-commerce maga-
zine. There are over 1,000 business magazines in the UK,
and it is reckoned you need a marketing budget of £700,000
to launch a new one. We had about £700.

I decided to launch it by spending a week living in a shop
window surviving off the internet. I started in my pyjamas,
with a credit card and computer in a shop window in
Sauchiehall Street in Glasgow.

I had a number of challenges to complete. I had to order
food (£40 from Iceland – lot of food, no freezer). I organised
a dinner party, I got a barber to come in, a six foot wooden
giraffe, pipe band and vintage Bentley. The only challenge I
failed was from my dear sister – to get a glass of ice.

I also drew quite a crowd. I had two drunks who adopted
me and would post sandwiches through the letter box every
day, I got my own stalker who would smile enigmatically,
and a group of night clubbers – one of whom shouted
something about a job she would give me if I let her in – I
couldn't quite work it out.

The main benefit of the week was of course the publicity.
I was in all the main papers (I got my three month old
daughter in the Sun), on TV, had a radio station actually in
the window with me, and about 1,000 emails a day. We also
got more subscribers than any other business magazine
launch in Scottish history.

Consistency: A famous French chef was asked the secret of his success. He answered:

> *'Excellence is the sum of many small things superbly done.'*

To reassure your clients, look after the little pieces. This doesn't have to mean big expense. Make sure your phones are answered consistently, your logo is applied consistently on letters, envelopes, signs, uniforms, and invoices.

> *Nextdoor.com design and manufacture doors. Despite them being a small business, you are immediately impressed by their professionalism. In their shop, all the staff wear the same outfits, the fitters have overalls with corporate branding, as do the vans which are always bright and clean. This gives great reassurance to customers that they are dealing with a professional outfit.*

Think American: When you get first-hand experience of American businesses, you realise that often it is not that they are miles better than everyone else, it is just that they are miles better at creating the impression they are.

Sure, modesty is an endearing quality in a date, but it doesn't work for companies. Get testimonials from every other client you work for. Try to get some 'big names' on your client base even if, say, you only sweep the IBM car park.

What name for your business?

Often the strongest thing about your business is you so you don't have to hide yourself

Given all that we have talked about here, ideally your company name will be an embodiment of your brand.

Don't worry if you've picked a name and it's not the most imaginative, it won't stop you. Tesco was named after the founder's wife, Tessa Cohen. However, the right name can give you an advantage.

Reassurance: If you are sure this will be a major factor in the success of your business, then it makes sense to pick a reassuring name. An estate agency wanted a name that implied Scottishness, wisdom and wealth – they picked: Stuart Wise Ogilvie. However, don't get too stuck on being safe – Branson has had no problem branding an airline Virgin.

If your brand is you: As we saw, you are your business's greatest asset, and there is merit in putting you as your company name. Many consultancies, whether advertising, legal or design are named after their founders. Be aware that you will then become the embodiment of this brand, which is fantastic if you are outgoing, but a possible worry if you are more retiring by nature.

Memorable: If reassurance or individual service is not the most important thing for your business, then go for something memorable. If you can make people smile or think deeply, they will remember your name. This will make your marketing so much easier. Here are some good examples.

An independent TV company called 'Extra Vegetables':

> *The founder had been on a TV shoot, and the producer was apparently really stingy with the expenses. That night in the bar they had a few extra drinks, and listed them all on the receipt as 'Extra Vegetables'.*

An event organiser called 'Let me hold your balls for you':

> *This was actually one of my first businesses. I got the work, but also received a few extra unexpected offers as well.*

An IT consultancy called '3 frogs':

> *Three frogs sit on a log, one decides to jump off, how many are left? Three – making a decision does not imply action. This consultancy's focus was in making IT projects actually happen.*

Caspian Woods

"Let me hold your Balls for you".

Flat 6
75 Broughton Street
Edinburgh
EH1 3RJ

Tel: 031 557 8549
Fax: 031 557 9151

CHAPTER 13

Your place or mine?

Your place or mine?

There is a well-known saying about location:

Q: What are the three most important secrets in a retail business?

A: Location, location and location.

The problem is that the expense of getting the right location for your business can be prohibitive. A recent programme on the coffee phenomenon in the UK found that only one chain was actually consistently profitable. In the massive land-grab to get the best locations, most of the chains ended up paying so much in rent that it all but wiped out profits.

Some tips for getting the right place

Become a destination store: If people are prepared to travel to you, then you don't have to be located in prime retail space. Clearly, this is not easy, and not for every business. It depends on how distinctive you make your business. People might travel a few miles for an award-winning restaurant, but not for a café.

Slaters Menswear has a policy of picking slightly out of the way retail spaces. They tend not be on the main streets, or if they are, they'll be up on the second floors of buildings. What distinguishes them is the absolutely first-class customer service they give. This has helped them grow to become one of the largest menswear retailers in the UK.

Is 'busy' enough? Many start-ups will choose their site by counting the number of people going past a particular unit at a given time of day. However, have you noticed in your town the 'white elephant' units that never seem to work for any business? Just because they are in a busy place, doesn't mean they'll work. There might be a huge footfall outside a busy train station. However, the chances are that most people are on their way home or dashing to work – they won't have time to sit down for a leisurely lunch.

Pay heed to the dictum:

> **If you want to open a restaurant, open it next door to a successful one**

Can the mountain come to Mohammed? Can you go direct to your customers rather than wait for them to come to you? If you have a sandwich business, why not deliver them direct to people's desks? Could you deliver your products by mail order, scooters, the phone or the web (see below)?

Co-partner: Consider opening up in other complementary places. Costa Coffee has opened units in bookshops, estate agents, banks and large offices.

> *One young entrepreneur opened a Japanese noodle bar in the spare area of a pub. Instead of rent and upkeep, they both share the profits. As a result, he has a massive captive clientele, less fixed costs and fewer of the worries of his own unit.*

Remote selling – e-commerce, phone and mail order

After the dot.coms, is e-commerce dead?

The dot.com party has well and truly ended, and we are now suffering from the hangover. The real tragedy is that many people are shaking their heads, saying 'never again' and dismissing e-commerce out of hand.

History should teach us otherwise. The railway revolution at the turn of the century heralded a similar investment boom, and an equally precipitous bust. However, after this initial over-exuberance, nobody can deny that the railways ('just another route to market' – as nay-sayers dismiss the internet) had a radical impact on trade, and transformed certain industries.

Ignoring websites as online brochures (which we cover in Chapter 17), e-commerce has great potential for small businesses. It might give you the chance to enter new markets (especially overseas), it might allow you to build a stronger online brand than larger competitors, or it could help you undercut competitors by streamlining your production process.

 Toolkit: **Sign-up free for the internet magazine we publish: www.nb-mag.com**

At the same time, e-commerce is not the only game in town. The telephone has revolutionised the insurance industry and mail order is making continual inroads in retail.

Is it right for your business?

As we looked at on Chapter 12, you have to be sure *exactly* what business you are in.

The internet was meant to be the death of retailers. This ignores the fact that for some types of goods, retail is therapy. This is why Waterstones was not killed off by Amazon. I use Amazon to search for specific titles that I can wait for, I go into Waterstones because it's a haven when I'm out shopping and I can wander aimlessly and walk out with completely random titles. Make sure you know exactly what needs you are satisfying for your customers.

Conversely, you might think that there are areas of your industry where retailers are not adding any value. This has happened to many brokers such as insurance, travel, and stockbrokers. You might be able to build a great business by giving customers a cheaper way of missing them out.

What to avoid if you are selling online

Having spent a week living in a shop window off the internet, I feel in a good position to rant about what to avoid in sites. There is a large problem of 'trolley abandonment' – people who get so fed up with a website purchase that they just give up. This is up to 50 per cent of purchasers in some big companies. This is people in the store, with their trolley full and wallet out, yet the rest of the experience frustrates them so much they walk out. The simple rule is KISS: Keep It Simple Stupid. It includes:

Avoid complex animation: Imagine: you go to your local shoe shop. You are stopped at the front door, and asked if you can wait a couple of minutes while they get ready. Then when you walk into the store they run around with flags welcoming you into the store.

Don't hide the till: Make your online ordering obvious and as simple as humanly possible. In particular, avoid:

Passwords: I don't need a secret password to walk into my local Tesco store, so why do so many sites require one? I understand where secure transactions are required, but it is too much to expect someone to provide one just for some editorial. I must have registered at hundreds of sites and there is a limit to how many memorable dates, places and names of pets that I can think of.

Make sure the shop doesn't fall apart: I'm glad that sounds so obvious. I am still amazed at the number of airlines whose sites have glitches, or crash. I got an email from one of Britain's leading airlines last week. The reply address includes the words 'black hole'. How reassuring is that?

Don't build it and assume they will come: Just because you have a catchy name and a funky site, the world will not beat a path to your door. Even throwing millions at advertising won't make this happen. The same rules of marketing apply. Push your customers to your site, make sure it appears high up in search engine rankings, get reciprocal links with other sites, put your web address on all correspondence.

Don't be seduced by the promises of technology

CHAPTER 14

Making sure your price is right

Making sure your price is right

Getting your price right is hugely important. A 10 per cent increase in your price can increase your profits by as much as 40 per cent.

Setting the right price should be a tricky process for you. This is because pricing, and the whole notion of 'worth', is a very emotional issue, and deeply rooted in assertiveness. People are worried about asking a fair market price for their product or service because deep down they have a misguided sense of their own self-worth.

To get round this whole emotional minefield, people (and far too many business books) rely on technical pricing solutions. The most obvious version is 'cost-plus' pricing. Simply, you add up all your costs and then stick a margin on the top. While very tempting and easy, it is wrong for a basic reason:

 The right price is what your customer is psychologically willing to pay for your product. Your costs only tell you if you have got a good deal from your suppliers

When publishing yearbooks, I realised I could make my books hardback, which would cost an extra £1 each, but as a result I could sell them for double the price – an extra £8. At the same time, my sales went up! People felt these were higher quality books and this was a small price to pay for keeping the memories of their friends and university safe for years to come. Which is also why I called the company 'Time of Your Life!'.

Six reasons not to be cheap as chips

There is nothing sadder in a business presentation than someone saying 'and we will win lots of customers by being the cheapest'. As well as implying something about the person's sense of self-esteem, it can cause a lot of business problems.

1. As a small business it's unlikely you will have the economies of scale (like purchasing power) to undercut everyone else indefinitely. You will probably only succeed in doing this by working yourself to the bone until you get complete burnout.

2. Don't forget, your competitors will react. If you start scooping up new customers, you run the risk of triggering a price war. They will probably have deeper pockets and more established customers than you, and anyway, no one will win.

3. Once you have established a low price with a customer, it is very difficult to raise the price later. Imagine trying to increase your price by 30 per cent with an existing customer – they'll turn round and say 'What kind of mug do you take me for?' The same applies with 'Sales' in shops – do it too often and customers will just sit tight knowing one will be along soon.

4. Bear in mind – customers have an irksome habit of talking to each other. If you drop the price for one, be very sure everyone else won't find out.

5. Low price and good value are not the same thing. Don't think that if you drop your price, customers will immediately beat a path to your door. Far more likely, they might think you are cheap and nasty and avoid you like the plague.

6. You risk ending up with just the cheap customers, who will dump you as soon as the price goes up.

   A number of hungry American credit-card companies came into the UK market keen to grab customers with zero-rate interest deals. The idea was that having hoovered up a big market share they could put their rates up. The problem was that they mainly got 'promiscuous' customers hungry for a good deal, who of course moved on to the next zero-rate deal when they put their rates up.

Some pricing strategies

Your customers should squeak at your price: This is an acknowledgement that while your price is uncomfortable, it is only uncomfortable because they still want it. You can then make them feel a little better about it by offering them a special discount such as free delivery or a free carrier bag. This allows the customer to feel better about the whole thing and convince themselves mentally that actually they've got a great bargain. (If they actually scream and run from the building then you've possibly gone a bit far.)

A great thing to point out to customers is:

> *You can have this good quality, you can have this fast, and you can have it cheap. You can have any two of these you choose, but you cannot have all three. Which do you want?*

See how elastic your customers are: An unusually sexy term from economics, 'elasticity' is a measure of how far you can push certain customers before they snap. You'd be surprised how far certain customers will go. Who would have thought we'd be happy to pay £2.50 for some coffee beans and hot water, or £20 for withered flowers at an airport? You will often find your most elastic customers where there is a deeper need you are meeting that you might not have realised (i.e. feeding an addiction in the case of coffee, or marriage guidance counsellor in the flower case). Look at Chapter 12 for 'Understand what business you are in'.

Set fire to your price list: Different people will pay different prices, in different places, in different seasons, at different times of the day, for a whole host of different reasons. People will pay double the price for a hardback book, mainly because they are desperate to read it before anyone else.

In an ideal world you would be able to price according to each and every customer's degree of need. This is, of course, fiendishly difficult to do and remember (though certainly doesn't mean you shouldn't try).

Start by trying different prices depending on the type of customer (i.e. a cheaper price to trade customers, than to ordinary punters). Then try different pricing for different geographical markets, then perhaps for timing.

> *As a small Scottish marketing agency, I once quoted a job for a friend in a big London-based agency. He phoned me*

up, chuckling 'Caspian you idiot, you've sent me your costs
– I need your prices'.

When you get more experienced in this, you can start to become a Jedi Price Master and read each customer coming through the door and price according to their level of desperation.

Don't win every customer: It is much better to have five customers paying you £20 an hour than ten paying £5.

Price your offering on what it saves your customers, not what it costs you

For example:

> *An oil services business specialised in stopping 'gushers' – whereby oil escapes uncontrollably from a well. They used to price their service on the cost of their travel and then an hourly rate for their service. A consultant pointed out that the cost per hour to the oil company of a gushing well was in the tens of thousands of pounds. The company therefore re-priced their offering based on how much their prompt action saved their customers.*

This explains why night plumbers charge so much.

Trade your customers up:

> *You can normally buy a beefburger from a fast-food joint for 99p, but can you remember the last time you actually did? They make their money by trading people up to the Super Dooper meals and Extra Everything or 'Go Fat', which is where they make the money while still keeping the impression they are cheap.*

Never underestimate your customers' willingness to trade up

Think how many times you have been tempted into a shop by a low price in the window, only to be sweet-talked by a salesperson, and end up leaving the shop weighed down with expensive goodies. This should be your policy.

An alternative, and I think slightly dishonest approach, is to hook customers with extras. Think of all the extended warranties you get in electrical shops. Ever wondered why buying refill razor blades is more expensive than buying the original razor? My view is you may get customers once, but they'll get wise.

Tell your customers to BOGOF: A variation on the previous strategy, this wonderful acronym in the retail trade means Buy One Get One Free. This, and its multiple variations (25 per cent larger, third one free, etc.) is a good way to allow customers to feel they've got a good deal, while keeping up the value perception of your product.

What if my industry is VERY price-sensitive?

There are precious few businesses that aren't pretty price-sensitive, and some that are chillingly so. Customers are savvy these days. So what can you do?

Specialise in a niche, not the mass market: It might be uncomfortable at first, but it can be far more pleasurable to have a small but highly profitable specialist niche in a market where you can keep your operations small, and lovingly craft your product.

> *The pressure of cheaper Chinese-produced shoes has eroded the UK shoe manufacturing industry. However, a growing number of small British manufacturers make a very good living from hand-crafted shoes sold around the world at up to £1,000 a pair.*

Add non-core items: See if your customers will pay more if you add extra benefits to your service such as delivery, specialist packaging, installation services or after-sales support.

Be entrepreneurial in finding supplies: Look hard at new technologies or new markets for getting suppliers.

Stress your added value: You might be able to justify a higher price if you can clearly demonstrate that you add more value than your competitors.

Get out: Maybe you've inherited a business, or started up in a trade you have always been in. Unfortunately, just because there was a future for your business yesterday doesn't mean there will be one tomorrow. However much we lament the hordes of industrious Chinese who will work fifty times harder for a bowl of rice, they aren't going to go away. There are 1.3 billion of them.

Perhaps you can find a new market where the competition is a bit less intense.

CHAPTER 15

Getting your customers

Getting your customers

You've got your idea, funding, marketing, premises. You are ready to get cracking. Now comes the important stuff.

 Sales are the single critical success factor in your business

Customers are the fuel for your spaceship. It doesn't matter how wonderfully packaged your product, how good your systems, how well kept your books. If you don't have any fuel, you're going nowhere.

Put aside the myth that if you build a better mousetrap, your customers will beat a path to your door. I met a business which is a very salutary example of this.

> *There is a group of four incredible boffins running a fabrics company. They have taken fabrics to an extreme level. In amongst high-tech medical fabrics and bandages, they have developed part of a propulsion system for the space shuttle, a new suspension system used on London taxis, they invented a new design for an airbag and the company which bought it kitted out an assembly line with 100 staff to mass-produce it. Yet, until recently they were living in an attic eking out a living. The reason? – they were not very good at selling their products.*

But before you rush out and leaflet the town, you need a logical and systematic approach. This is because of the importance of the number 4.

The magic number 4

I've got an old Renault, reasonable condition, looking for £1200, do you want it?

What, who, hey, hold on a second...

You cannot make someone buy something the first time they've heard of it. The one real nugget I got from four years of a business studies degree was being introduced to a lovely lady called AIDA. She works something like this...

- The first time someone hears about your business, they have **A**wareness
- The second time they hear this might have heightened to **I**nterest (or, better yet, they are **I**ntrigued)
- The third time they hear, they might have actual **D**esire for your product or service
- But only on the fourth contact will they finally take any **A**ction. This translates into the fact that:

> **80 per cent of sales come after the <u>fourth</u> contact you make with a prospect**

Many businesses make the mistake of putting a massive amount of money into one piece of marketing, like PR or press advertising, and then sit back to wait for the customers to roll in.

Someone might see your flyer sitting on their doormat, and register a vague awareness before stepping over it. Then they might read something about you in the local paper and actually have a desire to use your service, but still not pick up the phone. It is only when you give them a call that this turns to action, and they finally purchase your product.

So, whatever field your business is in, you need a sales funnel:

The sales funnel

Most classically trained sales professionals work with a sales funnel. As the name suggests, imagine a large funnel into which you start dripping not water but customers until the funnel starts to fill up, and they eventually come out the other end as sales.

Now, being canny entrepreneurs – why start at the wide end of the funnel – advertising, direct mail, websites which will take a few weeks/months/days to trickle down? No, let's start with the bit where we will get our quickest sales: people who already know and trust us.

Identifying your first leads

Unless you have very rich backers (or you are a dot.com), your sales approach should be that of a sniper and not a shotgun (apologies for the analogy but I couldn't think of a better one). Don't say, 'Well, my customers could be everyone'. That's very nice for your ego, but it's not much use in focusing your sales.

You need to identify who your most likely customers would be. These are people you can get to trust you quickest. These are people who already know you, or have worked with you, or who you know will trust you quickly. If you have no warm prospects like this, then you need to draw up a profile based on factors such as their location, their budget, their life stage.

You might also know customers from your competitor's business who might switch. OK, so that sounds a bit naughty, but this is business. For a start, you know these people have the budgets, and are interested in the product. There might be smaller customers your competitor is not as interested in. You never know – your competitor might even be interested in you taking them off their hands – stranger things have happened.

> ### ♟ Entrepreneur's Secret: Watch out for change
> A great number of products and services are bought during periods of change. This could be life change like moving house, or having a baby (a huge time for video camera sales). Alternatively, in company sales it could be when a new person takes over purchasing.
>
> Look for news stories, job announcements in the trade papers, even personal ads in the papers. Also look at other routes to these people. You could approach local estate agents and through them offer new house purchasers a free consultancy on gardening design.

CHAPTER 16

How to become a hot sales person without selling your soul to Lucifer

How to become a hot sales person without selling your soul to Lucifer

It is vital that you learn to how to sell.

Many famous entrepreneurs are mostly glorified hustlers. Marks & Spencer started as market barrow boys. Richard Branson started in a telephone box. However, don't worry if you are not a 'born salesperson'; you can learn to be good at sales.

Being a good salesperson does not require you to

- lose your morals and integrity
- have a personality bypass
- wear red braces.

However, there is one thing you will have to overcome:

Prepare yourself for rejection

Tom Farmer started his Kwik-Fit car servicing empire from a single business unit. One of his first sales approaches was to telephone large corporate buyers and sell to them. However, he found he got a high proportion of knock-backs. So he studied his approach – was it timing, was it his price, was it his competition? After trying lots of different approaches, he found that, no matter what, his ratio stayed at about twenty calls to every sale. So, he changed his attitude. 'I learned to stop worrying about all those noes and to get through them as fast as possible so I could get to the 'yeses.'

Don't worry if you'd rather eat your shoes than make a cold call to a stranger – so would most normal people. The reason we don't like selling is that we don't like personal rejection. Psychologists reckon we take around 50 per cent of our sense of identity and self-worth from what others around us tell us – no person is an island. If you are selling, you're going to encounter a fair bit of rejection. If you keep getting knocked back, you are going to feel miserable after a while. I think we all have a certain level of self-esteem – mojo if you like – and this goes up and down depending on feedback from others.

See Chapter 24 for a fuller guide to medicine for your mojo. In terms of selling – bear the following in mind:

> ## As any Casanova at your local nightclub will tell you: it's a numbers game

> *My best mate Paul snogged Carol Glaister. I'd fallen in love with her at about 13 years old, and worshipped her from afar throughout one hot summer. Then we went to the cinema with my mate Paul, and half way through they started snogging. I was heartbroken. The thing was – Paul was in the habit of asking girls and not really being fazed if they said no. And he looked like a monkey.*

You have to kiss a lot of frogs before you get your prince or princess. It's the same with selling. The secret is to take these rejections in your stride and **don't take them personally.**

The following are some ways to do this:

Keeping your pecker up

It's mostly a matter of timing

> *We did some research into why our customers had bought from us. Was it our cutting-edge thinking, our keen pricing, the fact we were all-round great guys? Time after time, our clients said 'Well, you just happened to call us at the right time'.*

Most sales come from being in the right place at the right time. I'm amazed at how many times I call people and they say, 'I was just thinking about calling you'. The thing is, they never do if you don't call first. It's worse when you call and they say 'If only you'd called last week, we've just bought something'.

Brace yourself – people will reject you. The secret is not to take it personally.

Try to make this work in your favour. Look to see if there are peak times in the day, year or month when people most want to buy from you and go hell for leather then.

Work out your numbers

Your job with sales is not always to be winning work, but it is to be moving people down your sales funnel. Work out what your ratio of success is. This will vary from business to business, but I'll give you mine:

- 1 out of 7 calls I make gives me a lead, or a meeting
- 1 out of 4 leads gives me a chance to quote
- We win 1 out of 3 jobs we quote for.

Therefore, each week, I work from a sales form which tells me how many calls I need to make, or how much work I need to bring in that week, or quote for.

The point of this is not to worry if work is not automatically coming in – so long as you are filling up your funnel with water, it will start to come out of the other end eventually.

Every week you will have a target. The point is once you have met your target, give yourself a break – you don't have to do any more for the rest of the week. Perhaps you've won a piece of work, or got some leads. Other weeks, you won't win any work, but will be keeping up your call level.

 Toolkit: **On the website there is a sales funnel template for you to work with: (www.fromacorns.com)**

And sometimes something spooky happens. I will have had a week of really busting my guts and getting nowhere. Then, at the end of the week, out of the blue, someone calls us with a totally unrelated piece of work. I think of it as sales karma.

Grasp the nettle

The dread of making your calls is always worse than the reality. My advice is to plunge straight in. Make your hardest couple of calls first. After this, you should be on a roll, so do all your other calls quickly while the momentum is there. Once you've made your target, have a break and feel very smug.

Reward yourself

Most professional sales outfits award sales bonuses as we are simple creatures and respond well to simple rewards. You should do the same for yourself. This can be either a pure cash bonus, or something else you've promised yourself like a CD, bottle of wine, or electronic gadget (my personal favourite).

Keep the bonuses to yourself. While a bit of strutting around after a sale is to be expected, coming in to work the next day on a new Harley-Davidson has a tendency to put other people's backs up.

Making a sales call

Get the right person (not the nice person)

The first step is to make sure you are speaking to the person who will ultimately make the decision to buy. This is harder than it sounds.

Imagine you have no purchasing power in your personal relationship (I know I don't). First, you might not actually realise this, and second, you are not going to admit this to a stranger.

Make sure you are selling to the person who really makes the decision

Sales calls are scary, and sometimes the temptation is to just call people you like and are nice to you. There is nothing worse than spending months building a relationship with someone who you belatedly find out has nothing to do with the purchasing decision.

To find out if you have got the right person, you might just have to be blunt. Ask them outright who will make the final decision, and whether it is worth speaking to them as well.

> ♦ **Entrepreneur's Secret: How to get past the gatekeeper**
>
> Many companies try very hard to keep people like you and me at bay. Often the gatekeeper will be a secretary. We once even had someone put on a funny voice pretending not to be themselves.
>
> The best way past them is with a referral. Get the name of anyone else in their department and say, 'Bob suggested I speak to them'. Don't be fobbed off with leaving a number and expecting them to call back – they won't. However, bear in mind that most purchasing decisions in big companies are not made by people at the top – perhaps you should aim a bit lower?

Understand what the objective of your call is

No one likes a pushy salesperson who tries to take you from an awareness of their product to giving out your credit card details in one five-minute call. Keep in mind AIDA. Your first call can simply be to find out who has purchasing responsibility. If you get hold of the right person, then you can do a brief fact-find before sending them some information on your business. It will then probably take a further call for a meeting, or even to close the sale.

Face-to-face selling

Despite the promises of technology, most sales still need to be done face to face.

In a sales meeting, remember:

 Your objective is not to talk people into buying something. It is to get them to talk themselves into buying it

To find out what they want, you are going to have to question. As a rule of thumb, you should not talk more than 50 per cent of the time.

This is very hard for someone enthusiastic. Imagine going on a first date and the person spouts endlessly about themselves – it'll be a lonely taxi ride home for them. Instead, you should follow the Leslie Phillips school of seduction: 'So pussy cat, tell me about yourself...'

1. Preliminary chat: Be careful with small talk prior to and after a meeting. You may see this as a chance to schmooze, but you can instantly get off on the wrong foot. I know of a salesperson who casually mentioned the previous night's football, got into a heated debate, and lost the sale before they'd even started. If anything, keep it innocuous, such as 'How's business?'

2. Introduction: You should start by establishing your 'bona fides'. If a complete stranger came up to you in a bar and started an inter-rogation, you might be a tad cagey. A simple start might be 'We have worked with xxx in your industry, won these awards, and have some great ideas of how we might be able to help you. However, before we do this, I need to know something about you'.

3. Fact find: You now need them to open up about their business, and what possible needs they have. To do this, you need to ask open-ended questions that get them talking, and not 'closed' ones that can be answered with just yes or no and so end your meeting:

Bad closed questions:	Good open questions:
Have you ever thought about...? ('No')	**What are** your main objectives?
How many products do you have? ('Six')	**Why** do you focus on this?
Do you buy from salespeople? ('No, goodbye')	**How do** you choose a supplier?

⚓ Entrepreneur's Secret: Find out the hidden agenda
The answers people give you initially are not necessarily the real answers. Every brief we get asks for 'creativity'. However, the buyer's greatest concern is usually being able to carry on paying the mortgage. What they often mean is 'give me something that is 99 per cent the same, but with a little twist'.

4. Present your benefits: At school, did you ever notice that if you directly quoted back to a teacher something they had previously said, your grades went up?

Your prospect should have just told you exactly what they want from a supplier. It is now a matter of you repeating back 'It's funny you should say that using a local company is important, I used to go to school up the road' etc.

Don't worry if this seems completely transparent and disingenuous. The beautiful thing about flattery is, no matter how obvious it is – we still love it.

5. Handle their objections: You now want to find out what are your prospect's problems with you.

As odd as it may sound – objections are good. Think back to your last big purchase – I bet before you took the plunge there were lots of things you wanted to ask and check up on. It shows you are serious about making a purchase, and just want some reassurance. If you can successfully answer your prospect's objections, they will have to give you the work.

 Toolkit: **The three main customer objections and how to handle them.**

The customer says:	What they mean:	What you say:
I'm happy with my current supplier	Loyalty	1. Don't slag the competition – you will undermine the person you are selling to. 2. Ask lots of questions about the competitor's service/ product. 3. Stress the difference of your offer. 4. Get them to consider a trial offer.
I can't see me needing that	Demand	1. Actively question them about why not. 2. Talk through your current customer base and why they use you. 3. Come back to them.
It's too expensive	Price	1. Question the client – 'What makes you say that?' 2. Get comparison with other products. 3. Question them on the benefits you offer and their need. 4. Stress the value you add and not the cost.

Don't go overboard with answers, and dig yourself into a hole. Answer succinctly and learn to shut up.

Don't say: 'No, don't be a fool'. Nod sagely and say 'It's interesting you should say that, what we found in fact was...'

Don't rubbish the competitors – it belittles you, and belittles the buyer. Do, however, be sure to be patronising about them at *every* opportunity.

6. Close the sale: I used to think it was somehow rude to ask for the business. I would have fantastic meetings and practically become life-long buddies with my prospective clients, but never actually ask them for the business.

The simplest way is to wait until they have run out of objections, and then ask: 'Can we have your business?'

This may sound incredibly stupid, but like many stupid things it can work very well. Quite often, the person will be surprised, and say 'Yes, OK then'. If not, at least they will tell you what other objections they have which you can then counter.

> 🔦 **Entrepreneur's Secret: Don't be afraid of silence**
>
> If you are dealing with a professional buyer, they will often have been trained to use silence as a way of intimidating you into dropping your price. Be prepared to shut up. Repeat a rhyme in your head if it helps (though try not to let your lips move at the same time as this can be a bit disconcerting). I have heard of two professional salespeople who sat silently looking at each other for a couple of minutes before one of them blinked.

7. Beware of slack chat: You've closed the sale, you are on your way out. Don't blow it all by some random comments as you walk out of the door.

> *I had sold someone an insert into one of our magazines. At the end of the call I said 'Err...well, I look forward to inserting it for you' and hung up. There was a deathly hush around me as my colleagues stopped their work and looked up at me open-mouthed.*

CHAPTER 17

How to get more customers

How to get more customers

OK, so you have your first customers? Now you have to put a three-point plan in place to nurture these customers so that they become the foundation of your business.

Step One: Keep your customers loyal

There is no point busting a gut winning new customers if your existing customers just walk out of the door. Many surveys show that the average company will lose 50 per cent of their customers every four years.

As well as repeat business, loyal customers have other benefits:

- They will often pay higher prices because they trust you (and you know how much you can get away with charging them!)
- It is easier to sell them additional things
- They cost less to service – you know what they need, and they know what you supply.

There has been a lot of hype about so-called loyalty cards, points and schemes. This is hogwash. As a French loyalty expert said:

'You cannot keep your lover loyal by giving them points, and then offering to double them if they stay until break-fast.'

As a result, the most frequent business flyers are 'loyal' to an average of four different airlines – they join all the schemes and get the points regardless.

Customer loyalty isn't rocket science – it's just a matter of showing them the love.

'Sixty per cent of customers who leave a supplier do so not because of price, or a better product, but simply because of a lack of care and attention from their old supplier.'

Give your customers a call or visit on a regular basis (not just when a pitch is coming up) – even if it's just to see how they're getting on. Take them out for a meal if you can afford it. Produce a simple newsletter giving them helpful advice, and updates on your business. Send them a card on their birthday, or a bottle at Christmas. And don't just think about the person at the top. The MD's secretary might be the most important person in the company for you!

🏆 Entrepreneur's Secret: If you lose a customer, swallow your pride

I know from bitter personal experience, when you lose a customer it's very tempting to start howling and throw all your toys out of the cot, but that doesn't change anything. Try to treat this as just a delayed opportunity.

1. Find out why you lost out. Chances are, they'll feel a bit bad for saying 'no' to you, so they should be prepared to give you honest and constructive feedback on what you could do better next time.

2. While they're still feeling bad, ask if there is any other work coming up or anyone else in the organisation you should speak to.

3. Keep in touch with them. They are still a hot prospect for you – their current supplier might cock-up. Put a 999 plan in operation – phone them 9 days, 9 weeks, and then 9 months after you lost the work. If their relationship gets into trouble, it will often do so at these stages, and this is a good chance to step in.

Step Two: Sell more stuff to your loyal customers

 It is five times easier to sell to an existing client than it is to a new one

If you have sweated blood to get in with a new client – keep selling to them. Go back to them and sell them other products and services. Think laterally about what these services might be. They obviously liked you enough to buy it the first time, so there's no reason why they shouldn't continue to buy.

> *Alistair Rutherford co-founded Edinburgh Preserves originally selling chutney made from his grandmother's recipe. On the success of this, they now produce over twenty different varieties of chutneys as well as mustards, relishes, and pudding sauces to supermarkets around the UK. If you think this is a ridiculous number of chutneys – look at a Heinz ketchup bottle – it says 57 varieties on the side!*

Step Three: Build word-of-mouth marketing

Wouldn't it be great if people loved your business so much they told their friends, and their friends told their friends? It can and does happen, and should be something you should strive for in your business. Referrals are much more likely to lead to a sale because people trust their friends. Of course, it's not easy, and the following are some starting points:

- Ask for referrals. Make it a habit after you have delivered a good service for a customer to ask them if there are three other people they know who might be interested. You can either wait for them to pass on the good word, which is great (if it actually happens). A quicker method is to say 'Is it OK if I talk to them and mention your name?'
- Let your customers know how valuable referrals are for you. Stress this in meetings, put it in your literature and on your website.
- Give people an incentive for referrals. You could be blunt and

offer them a 10 per cent discount on their next purchase, or a bottle of bubbly. Quite often it's just recognition – phone them up and say 'Thanks for the lead, it looks promising and means a big deal for us' – it will give them a lovely warm glow, and a greater willingness to refer in future.

- Viral marketing. This horrible term comes from the internet, where people forward funny website links and emails. It's a good general principle, however. Make it easy for people to refer you. Give people things they can pass on, such as a stock of cards, stickers, newsletters, brochures, or just a simple website address. Anything that makes it easy to say 'Hold on, I've got her number here…'

- Identify your star referrers. Keep track of who is your best source of sales leads. They might not actually be a client – they could be a supplier, the head of a trade body, or your bank manager. Be nice to them!

- Keep in touch. How many times have you found yourself saying to someone 'Funnily enough, I was talking to someone about this the other day…'? Consider a newsletter or just regular updates on your progress.

🕴 Entrepreneur's Secret: Encourage people to complain

You will probably have heard the saying that while a happy customer might tell one other person, an unhappy customer will tell around five others. But interestingly, research by the Bank of Scotland found that the customers who complained the most were actually their most loyal customers. If you can resolve a problem with a customer to their satisfaction, they will trust you more in future, and will be more likely to tell others about the positive experience.

So, get customers to give you their feedback. Have comment boxes for customers, and take the effort to ask people how happy they are with your product. Don't simply rely on them telling you because they may just seethe in silence, and then spread the bad word.

Other promotion

OK, you have a bedrock of loyal customers who are spreading the good word, now you want to start filling up the funnel with some more leads.

The temptation now is to do lots of other marketing and promotion – advertising, brochures, websites, PR, direct marketing and the like. The main reason? It sure beats having to call them directly.

> **Promotion is no replacement for personal selling**

You should only consider doing any of the following as a *supplement* to your sales effort, as detailed in the next chapter.

Direct marketing

In direct marketing, a personal touch can make all the difference

This has got a bad name. The problem is that you are often trying to get from awareness to action in one move. Even the largest companies typically only get a response rate of 1–2 per cent. If you are lucky, the other 98 per cent either don't see your mailer or just ignore it and won't get upset with you bombarding them with junk mail.

If you are going to do direct marketing, then here are some tips:

- Follow up your mailing with a call. Remember AIDA? Your hit rate will go up considerably if you call people to see what they thought of your offer.
- Make sure your database is good. If possible, do a quick call first to check the contact details are right. While you are at it, why not ask if they are the right person to send information to – you will already be two steps up your sales funnel.
- Do a trial run with a limited number first, and get someone external to your business to proofread it for glaring mistakes that are so easy to miss.

    A marketing company was running a campaign targeting wealthy investors. A temp in the office had been playing around with the system, but no one did a test of the campaign before sending the letters off. The envelopes were fine, it's just that they all contained a letter which started 'Dear capitalist pig'.

- Make it different: This is the golden rule we keep coming back to.

It's a noisy world out there, and if you want to get noticed, you've got to stand out from the crowd. Don't, however, follow the example of one company who recently stuck thousands of flyers designed to look like parking tickets under car windscreen wipers – doh!

Do I need a brochure or website?

Your business might sell directly via the web. That's fine, and something we've covered in Chapter 13.

However, many websites fall into the category of 'brochure-ware'. And, like a brochure, they can be filed under the heading of 'things to distract you when you should be out selling to people'.

Companies can spend a fortune on websites (again, another area where large companies don't have a monopoly on common sense), in the hope that people will beat a path to their door. Fat chance. There are no short cuts in selling – you are going to have to do a lot of pushing to get prospects there in the first place.

Where brochures and websites can work is in reassuring prospective clients. See the section on branding for the importance of this. However, remember that you can reassure people very quickly and simply, so don't build a website unless you really need to, and don't spend a fortune on it (whatever the techies tell you).

PR

Getting a mention in the press can be valuable. It is probably cheaper than advertising, and more credible. It can also build the good buzz around you, and reassure customers. Vitally, it can also be hugely satisfying to the old ego (unless it is under the 'Court Appearances' section).

Tips for getting a mention in the press: Journalists are human (despite what some people might tell you), so:

- Don't rely on blanket press releases. As with every type of selling, there is no replacement for picking up the phone and calling them directly.
- They want to see a small business do well, particularly up against a big company. Don't play down the emotions of your story.
- If you've got a sympathetic contact, nurture them. Keep them posted with your good news, and if they run a good story – send

them a bottle of wine as a thank-you.

An employee of the Prince's Scottish Youth Business Trust took a journalist from one of the national papers out for a lunch. Over the next year, he ran six half-page spreads on PSYBT businesses. An initial outlay of £32 brought in tens of thousands of pounds of good publicity.

 Toolkit: Visit the website for a sheet of advice on writing a good press release: (www.fromacorns.com)

- A good eye-catching photo can be better than a long press release. *Quite often newspapers will scout around for an appealing photograph to take up space on the news pages. If you want to get in to the paper you should also ask to speak to the picture desk, as well as the journalists.*

Advertising

Advertising is an easy way to blow a lot of money very quickly. Remember AIDA – people won't buy your product/service the first time they hear about it. If you are going to advertise, make sure it is very focused, and backed up by lots of other selling and promotion.

Again, try to make it different. Ideally, rather than just interesting your prospects, a good piece of advertising will *intrigue* them. You are then much closer to a sale. Being eye-catching and funny doesn't require a huge spend on advertising.

I recently saw a leather coat store with the sign: 'Due to an expensive divorce, Mr Toskana is having to sell his stock fast'. The cost of the sign must be a few pounds, but it is seen, and probably remembered, by thousands of people each day.

♟ Entrepreneur's Secret: Don't be talked into taking advertising by good salespeople

Make sure you have a plan and stick to it. To illustrate my point – how do these people sell advertising space to punters? Do they stick ads in magazines hoping you'll read them? Of course they don't. They pick up the phone and call you.

Networking/Notworking

This is the fine art of mingling with prospective customers at an event, or golf course, to get work from them. For this reason it is also known as Notworking.

Done well, and with the right people, you can move a person the whole way from awareness to action in the course of a five-minute chat. There are many forums where you can meet prospects: Chambers of Commerce, local business clubs, industry forums. However, before attending each one, carefully consider whether you will actually meet many of your potential customers there.

Partnering

There is a fantastic book called '*Marketing Judo*' by the team who took a local fish and chip restaurant, Harry Ramsden's, into a global brand. Their philosophy is that small nimble companies can achieve huge success by partnering with large established businesses.

There are many different ways you can do this:

- It could be by enticing a local celebrity to eat in your restaurant, giving you excellent publicity, in return for perhaps one free meal.
- You can do it on a small scale. For example, a local sports team might promote your sports shop if you provide them with free shirts.
- Alternatively you can do it on a huge scale.

  Richard Tait had designed and developed a new board-game called Cranium. However, his business only had four staff, and he didn't have the clout to get into the big game retailers. Instead, he knew someone at Starbucks. They were looking for other items to sell which could complement their brand. They took Cranium on, first locally, and then nationally. It became, after café lattes, one of their fastest selling items. Then one night on the Oprah Winfrey Show, Julia Roberts mentioned how she loved playing the game. Sales went through the roof.

CHAPTER 18

Your growth strategy

Your growth strategy

It is essential that your business plan is not consigned to the bottom drawer for a laugh in a few years as you sit

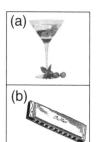

(a) on your yacht sipping a martini

(b) on the underground busking with a rusty harmonica
     (delete as appropriate).

It is time to start thinking about your strategy.

I know this seems a big word for a small business, but even if you only sketch out your thoughts on the back of a fag packet, it is vital you keep rethinking where your business is going. A common problem is:

> 💡 **Small business owners spend too long in the engine room and not enough time on the bridge**

If the story of Shell at the start of the book says anything, it is how successful businesses have to change and adapt to customer demand. Consider the following:

> *Not long ago, an accountancy graduate from Strathclyde University found himself unable to get a job. He'd been turned down by the major firms, and a number of minor ones as well. He therefore decided to start a business from his dad's garage. He thought there was a market in training shoes. With tongue in cheek, he wrote to a number of department stores stating he was a fast expanding footwear company and asked for space in their stores. Three of them accepted, and for many months he would drive around the country delivering to these, and catching a few hours of sleep in the back of his old van amongst the shoe boxes.*

It worked, and with time he built this to concessions in about forty stores. Only then did he decide to open his first own brand Sports Division store. Things carried on well, and in 1995, he seized the chance to buy the ailing Olympus Sports. Three years later Tom Hunter sold his business for £290 million, of which he pocketed £260 million.

When talking about his strategy, Tom says: 'I never had a definite goal in mind when I started out, I just wanted to grow. There is a certain logic to business and our attitude was to take things one thing at a time and see what developed'.

Some simple planning tips

The following are important things with your strategy:

Be single-minded about your customers' needs: If this sounds obvious to you – good. Because there are an awful lot of companies (particular IT) that fall into the trap of what the SAS call 'Shiny Kit Syndrome'. They become infatuated with how lovely and shiny their product is and completely lose sight of why a customer needs it in the first place. And bear in mind, these needs can change quickly. So, a good strategy starts with a check on asking your customers what they would like in an ideal world.

In successful companies, strategy often comes from the front line, not the board room. No one is closer to the customers than the cashier who serves them. Who better to ask what they actually want?

Watch out for The Law of Unintended Consequences: The late great Douglas Adams, author of the *Hitchhiker's Guide to the Galaxy*, coined this law. He astutely observed how many technologies, and companies, end up doing almost the complete opposite of what they were intended to do.

For example, the PC came out of the space programme, the internet was designed as a civil defence network in the event of nuclear war (and is now ironically one of the greatest threats to national security!). The BBC was set up by a bunch of wireless manufacturers to flog more of their radios. More recently, look at mobile phones – a fortune has been spent on whizzy 3G technology, but the greatest growth has been in fiddly and clunky text messaging. The danger is that you spend too long locked in your laboratory creating your master invention, without checking what customers might actually want.

Give yourself time and space to get it wrong: It is highly unlikely you will immediately hit upon what your customers want, so start your business on the cheap, and give yourself time to find what your customers *really* want.

Share your plan: There is nothing like having to explain your plan to someone else to make it clear in your own mind. Don't catch yourself saying, as so many start-ups do:

> *I don't want to tell people my idea is as they might steal it and go and do it themselves.*

Remember success is 1 per cent inspiration, 99 per cent perspiration. Don't overestimate how brilliant your idea is nor underestimate how lazy other people are.

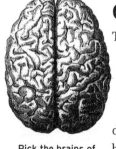

Getting good advice

To quote the entrepreneur Gio Benedetti:

> '*Starting a business is often like trying to climb a Scottish mountain in your shorts and flip-flops with just a road map to guide you.*'

In starting a business, you are entering a very strange country. It doesn't have to be like that. Millions of people have been there before you. Many of them will have had similar businesses. Even those in completely different businesses will often have some valuable insight. There is no doubt in my mind:

Pick the brains of someone who has been there before you

> **Getting advice from an experienced entrepreneur is worth its weight in gold**

Such a person is typically called a mentor, and is someone you *definitely* want to have. So, how do you get one?

How to hunt a mentor

Stage One: Draw up a mental job description for the person. Think of the experience and the type of advice you need. Is it general advice about how to build a business from scratch, or is it insight into your specific industry or your local target market? For example, if you are setting up a café, chatting to someone who has set up a clothing shop in your local area might tell you more than someone who has run a McDonald's franchise in a completely different part of the country.

Stage Two: Once you have a good idea of your dream mentor – ask around. Ask your family, bank manager, chamber of commerce, suppliers, business support organisations (see Appendix), clients. Even if it seems impossible, bear in mind the law of the Seven Degrees of Separation – a theory that everyone in the world can be linked together in seven steps. Someone will know someone who knows someone. You just have to be clear about what you want.

Stage Three: Convince them to come on board. This is not just a matter of cash and how much time they have free – most of the best mentors will want to do it if you can really sell them on your dream. There are, however, some rules.

- Don't be afraid to ask: I am amazed at how many successful entrepreneurs say they would love to help out a young business, but no one ever asks them. Entrepreneurs almost invariably have large egos, and love to have them polished by passing on their wisdom to young acolytes.

    When starting out with his mobile phone business DX Communication, Richard Emmanuel wrote a letter to Sir Tom Farmer, founder of Kwik-Fit asking for advice. He was startled when he received a prompt reply asking him in for a chat. They have since collaborated on a number of business ventures. Despite being one of Scotland's most successful businessmen, Sir Tom said people rarely ever asked him for advice.

    (It would probably be a wise idea if we all don't immediately pick up the pen now to him.)

- Don't ask for them for money.
- Don't take up too much of their time. If someone is successful, his or her scarcest resource will be time. Don't try to overly formalise the relationship, and don't demand too much too often: 20 minutes worth of advice over a pint from a good entrepreneur can be worth 3 hours of advice every week from someone else. Similarly, don't bog them down with the small stuff – ask them the big strategic questions.

Why just stop at one? There is no reason why you shouldn't get a range of mentors. A relative or a friend might be a good sounding board, as well as someone in your industry, and someone who has built a business. You will often find the greatest benefit is taking regular time to sit and think about your business and try to explain it to someone else.

Getting advice from professionals and consultants: If you can get such great advice free, the temptation is to wonder why you would ever pay for it.

Experts, whether lawyers, designers, management, marketing or employment consultants, often get a bad press. It is not so much that there are bad consultants as bad ways to use them.

You cannot get enough wisdom or good advice. They have often had years of experience in a particular area and can save you months of fiddling round. You should therefore be prepared to pay them accordingly.

The problem is when they become part of the furniture, and you just rely on them as a (very expensive) crutch for making decisions.

Always use the best advisers you can, but use them sparingly and for what they are best at. When they have imparted their wisdom – get them out. This isn't overly harsh, as any consultant worth their salt will be keen to get on to their next customers anyway.

CHAPTER 19

Keeping hold of your cash

Keeping hold of your cash

Cash is king

So now perhaps your business is up and running, and you are making profits. It's time to have a check on your cash position.

There is a big difference between profits and cashflow. There are many stories of fantastic businesses who have great products, good profits, and customers lined up, but go bust simply because they don't have enough cash in the bank for a short period.

Your cash can get eaten up by customers not paying in time (or at all), too much stock, or too much spending on equipment and overheads. Ironically, it is often businesses that are growing fastest who are at most risk from this problem – technically known as 'overtrading'.

Good cashflow will not make your business a success, but one thing is sure:

 Lack of attention to cashflow can break your business faster than almost anything else

So how do you stop this happening to you?

The ten golden commandments of getting paid

You have to learn to watch your cash like a hawk. Unfortunately, there are quite a few dodgy business people out there, and they can play havoc with a new-start business. Remember, if something sounds too good to be true, it probably is.

> **Until that money is in the bank (*and* the cheque has cleared), you haven't sold anything**

1. Open your bank statements

At every stage of your business, you should have a strong sense of how much cash you have in the bank and what the next month will look like. Don't stick your head in the sand and try to ignore this. Of course, you need proper books (which we are coming to), but your cash position should always be at the back of your mind.

2. Hire a dragon

It must be someone's clear responsibility in the business to chase up your overdue accounts, and you need a system for doing this. If there is only you, make sure you set aside a regular time each month to do this. Consider getting a book-keeper (see Chapter 20) to do this or an outside agency – see below.

Excellent for cash management

3. Don't automatically give credit:

When I produced my first yearbook, I was a penniless student but turned up to pick up the book from the printers with the cash in my briefcase. Strangely, nobody asked me for the money, and I kept my mouth shut. They automatically gave me thirty days' credit. I couldn't believe it. Fortunately for them, I didn't immediately spend it on beer, but kept the money in an account and paid them later, but I made a mental note to myself not to extend credit to my customers unless I absolutely had to.

Giving credit to people is exactly the same as lending them money. Just think how many new clients you would be happy to do this for. In fact, think about how many friends and members of your family you'd do this for!

4. If a new client demands credit, and you are nervous about them

- Ask them for some trade references and check them out. If they cannot provide them, that should raise some questions.
- Ask them for a deposit or a first stage payment for work in

progress. That usually sorts out the time-wasters.

- Don't place large orders with suppliers on behalf of new customers. Their non-payment can put you out of business at a stroke. Let them place the order directly with the supplier. You can always convince them of the discount they will get by going direct. In the longer term, you can do this for them.

5. Invoice in stages

If you deliver a service or product that takes a while to complete – invoice in stages from the start of the job. Our terms are a third on commencement of the job, a third on sign-off and a third on delivery. This greatly improves cashflow.

6. Negotiate

Negotiate payment terms with as much gusto as you negotiate price:

A business owner was selling to a big supermarket. After they had shaken on the deal, and he was packing up his bags, they brought up payment. Their standard terms were to pay in <u>90 days</u>. If they were to pay in 30 days, they would charge him 10 per cent of the cost. Imagine that – charging someone to pay them! That has got to be good.

7. Don't wait

Old debts are harder to collect, so don't wait 90 days before chasing overdue bills. As soon as an invoice is past your credit terms, institute your credit control procedure:

8. Pester power

Many companies operate a policy of not paying until shouted at. Learn a lesson from toddlers – the person shouting loudest will get served first. You should have a procedure similar to the following:

1. Phone up. Ask the person politely when you can expect payment (quite often they will have been waiting for a call before authorising payment). Often, they will fob you off ('it's in the post', 'our cheque run is next week'). In which case:

2. Keep them at their word. If they said 5 days, phone back then and ask where it is. Keep doing this until they keep their word. If you get no progress then:

3. Send a '7 day letter'. A lawyer or debt collection firm will be able to do this for a small sum. They will send a legal letter hinting at dark consequences if you don't pay within seven days. This acts as a very persuasive memory jogger!

4. If they are still not paying, you can seek recourse to lawyers or the small claims court. However, at this stage, you have to be honest with yourself whether they are ever going to pay. You could spend a large amount of time and money in an attempt to salve your pride. Better sometimes just to chalk it up to experience, and tighten your credit policy.

Some companies have turned pestering into an art form. A big London advertising agency sends a scruffy, smelly, and frankly menacing courier round to sit in the plush reception area of their clients until he is handed a cheque. In France apparently there is the 'payment chicken' you can hire – someone dressed in a chicken costume who follows the cheque signee around until they are paid.

Be prepared to use unorthodox methods to get people to pay

9. Don't rely on regulation

There are now well-meaning regulations allowing you to charge interest on late payment of bills, and many people put this on their invoices. I haven't heard of a single person who has made this stick. Are you prepared to take your customer to court over this? If they aren't going to pay you, then this clause is unlikely to help.

10. Consider invoice discounting/factoring

This involves signing over all your invoices to someone (usually the bank) for them to chase up. They pay you an immediate amount, and then the balance – minus their commission – when the bill is settled. This used to be a sign of a company in trouble, but it now has a much better image, and a much politer approach to collecting amounts. Some of our suppliers use this, and I think it is a sign of good management.

and while you're at it…

Join the club

This is terrible to say, but you don't want to be great at paying your suppliers if no one is paying you. So, with the following provisos, institute a policy of not paying until you have been paid.

> *A foundry business was experiencing a tight cash squeeze. The MD told his book-keeper to write out 63 cheques for all his creditors, but to lock them in a safe until they phoned up for payment. A couple of months later, his position was better, and he asked the book-keeper about the cheques. Fifty seven were still in the safe.*

Provisos:

- Always pay individuals and your smallest suppliers on time. Possibly, like you, this is their only income. If you don't pay them – they won't eat.
- Always pay your key suppliers promptly. You want a good working relationship with them. If you never pay them, they're not going to pull out the stops to do a good job for you.

CHAPTER 20

Aunty Nan's guide to keeping your books

Aunty Nan's guide to keeping your books

Don't be deceived by the charming exterior - the tenacity of a Rotweiller lies within

Most entrepreneurs are terrible at figures. It is quite rare to find a natural salesperson who is also a natural accountant. While well-kept books will not make you a success, giving them little or no attention can bring down an otherwise successful business.

We were very lucky in our early days to find a brilliant book-keeper – Aunty Nan – who has been keeping books all her life. This section is put together in the simplest way possible with her canny advice.

I strongly recommend that you employ a book-keeper. It needn't cost the earth – a few pounds an hour for an afternoon a week. It may seem like a cost in the short term but when those cheques roll in, it will be well worth it.

However, it is important that you learn the fundamentals of keeping your books. Think of it as time invested now in learning a new skill that will be useful throughout your life.

Basic book-keeping

Keeping good books is not rocket science. The golden rule when setting up a system is that it should be simple and methodical.

Do I need a software package? There is no reason why you shouldn't do your books by hand with a simple accounts book. However, there is a range of simple software packages that can help. The most important thing is to get the simplest you need. I used Quickbooks and Sage Instant. Don't go for anything more advanced unless you really need to. It will be easy to upgrade your system as time goes on.

Step One: Keep a record/invoice of each sale

You need to keep an invoice or a receipt for everything you sell.

File these in a ring-bound file in numerical order. When something is paid – write 'paid' at the top, and the date and cheque number. You will need a new file for every year.

Step Two: Keep a receipt of everything you purchase

Keep receipts for everything you buy. And I mean everything – parking tickets, petrol receipts, cups of tea, magazines, newspapers etc.

Make sure you ask for a 'VAT receipt' (i.e. one that shows the VAT number). Many places such as restaurants and petrol stations don't automatically give them. A credit card receipt is not a VAT receipt.

Put a number on every receipt (in the order you received them). Put these in a file called 'Purchases'.

Not everything can be claimed back against tax. See the next chapter on tax for a rough idea of what you can and cannot claim.

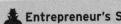 **Entrepreneur's Secret:** If in doubt, claim for it.

Step Three: Enter these in your records book

Enter the details of your sales and purchases in your records book.

For your sales, you need to record:

The date, the sale or invoice number, the customer name, the amount (including VAT). If you are registered for VAT, you will also need to include the amount of VAT, and the total without it.

For your purchases, it is a bit more complicated. You will record:

The date received, the name of the supplier, the number you've given it, the amount including VAT. If you are registered for VAT, you will also need to note the amount of VAT, and the total without it.

The next columns detail the nature of what you purchased. You can make these up depending on your most common purchases. Typically, you might include a brief breakdown of your direct supplies, and your overheads.

Step Four: Make sure these match your statements

So you've got all your records organised, and entered into your books. Now comes the hard bit. You have to go through your bank statement and check that the reality of what has come in and out of your account actually matches your beautiful books. This is important as it is the one time you can catch any glaring mistakes in your book-keeping.

Every cheque you have written has to be accounted for. If there is a payment from your account that you don't have a receipt for, you have to make a note of this in your books.

Cash

While obviously lovely to hold, real-life cash actually makes your books a bit fiddly. For all sorts of reasons that we have covered and will cover, you don't want to get into the habit of putting cash from customers into your back pockets if it was your own, and paying for business expenses out of your current account.

One solution is to use a credit card for your business expenses.

An alternative is to have a petty cash box. You can use this to pay for small purchases *providing* you keep a clear record of what you put in and take out of this box. The emphasis is from Nan, and I can tell you, if our petty cash box is out by 50p, it's like the Spanish Inquisition in our office!

Using an accountant

Ideally, a good accountant should save you more money than they cost. However, this depends partly on finding a good accountant, but perhaps more on using your accountant in the right way.

The following are some of the wrong ways to use an accountant:

✗ Don't get an accountant to do all your day-to-day book-keeping for you. A good book-keeper will be far cheaper (an accountant should be able to recommend one).

✗ Don't turn up at the end of the year with a big shoe-box full of hundreds of dog-eared bits of paper you have been filing under the bed. They will possibly be able to make some semblance of order from this, but it's unlikely to be 100 per cent accurate, and it will be very expensive.

✗ Don't get your accountant to produce your business plan for you. It is vital you 'own' and understand everything in your plan. If necessary, get some help with more complex financial aspects – but it has to be your plan.

✗ Don't try to do everything and complete all your year-end tax, allowances, depreciation and so on. Well, OK, you can, but it's unlikely you will get it all right. And hey, life's too short and it's sunny outside.

✗ Don't just speak to them when things are too late. Seek their knowledge early on in your start-up process to get advice about what legal form your business should take, when you should pick your tax year, the types of expenses you should claim and so on.

It is far better that you keep methodical and simple records, and present them to the accountant at the end of the year for them to weave their special accountant's magic with them.

How to get a good accountant: The best way has to be a recommendation. Go along to business networking events (see the appendix: Useful sources of information) and ask successful business people in similar types/sizes of business who they use. Alternatively, ask business support organisations, your bank manager or lawyer for a recommendation.

CHAPTER 21

Tax

Tax

You won't like it, but you've got to brace yourself – at some stage you are going to have to pay tax.

It is important to understand the tax implications for your business, even if you get an accountant to complete your tax return. Don't worry, it makes my head bleed as well, but get a nice cup of tea and sit down. I'll try to make this as painless as possible.

This section is not an exhaustive guide to tax regulations. That would take up far too much space in relation to its actual importance in the success of your business. Rather, I'll give you nuggets of wisdom and point you in the direction of more detailed advice. The Inland Revenue have an excellent guide on the tax issues for people starting in business. You can get it from: **www.inlandrevenue.gov.uk/startingup/index.htm** or by calling 08459 15 45 15.

Income tax

What you have to consider when starting out:

The legal form of your business

As we looked at in Chapter 11, you have to make a choice about the legal form your business will take. As well as all the other considerations, tax will play a part in your thinking.

Basically, if you are a sole trader, then you are taxed as an individual – all the profits of the business are taxed in the same way as if this was a straight salary.

With a limited company, your business is a separate legal entity. Even if you own all the shares, you are an employee of the business. You will therefore have to pay normal tax on your salary. On top of this, the company will pay corporation tax on its profits.

Moving from employee to start-up

There are a number of factors you should consider.

If you make a loss in your first year of trading, you might be able to claim back tax you have paid in previous years as an employee.

You should also check to see if you qualify for any government tax credits. Contact 0845 300 3900 or visit **www.inlandrevenue.gov.uk/taxcredits**.

Cashflow and tax

An unplanned for and unexpected tax bill can cripple a small business. This is not the fault of the Inland Revenue – it is the fault of the business for not anticipating it.

It is a hard discipline to learn if you have been previously taxed at source as an employee. Get into the habit of putting money by throughout the year to pay your tax bill. You can also pay your tax in instalments throughout the year.

What you can and can't claim for against tax

Ask your accountant for detailed advice about this, but here is a rule of thumb:

Can claim:

✔ A proportion of your home costs if you are working from home. This needs to be a distinct room that is solely used for your business. You can then claim a proportion (based on the total number of rooms in the house) of heat, light, phone, insurance, cleaning. You can also claim part of your mortgage but check first as you might find yourself hit for business rates.

✔ Business gifts (up to a limit), but not food and drink.

✔ Work travel.

✔ Subsistence (i.e. cost of food when away on work business).

✔ Relevant books, magazines, newspapers (including the Sunday ones for all-important 'research').

✔ Staff entertaining – up to a limit.

✔ The cost of employing your wife or husband (if you can demonstrate the work they actually do, and you're paying them the going rate).
Cannot claim:

✘ Your own income and living expenses.

✘ Client entertaining and meals

✘ Travel to and from your place of work.

✘ Clothing, i.e. suits

✘ Parking tickets and fines.

I have known some people who have really taken the mickey with this. A friend put her top of the range home hi-fi system through the business books as she claimed it was solely to play training videos and tapes for her staff. Another would once a year find that an essential work exhibition just happened to occur at holiday time, and in a warm sunny country, so of course he could put the trip, and associated essential fact-finding, through the business.

Of course, I couldn't possibly condone such behaviour nor encourage you to see if you could do likewise.

> **⚖ Entrepreneur's Secret: Bear in mind, the official term is 'wholly and exclusively for business use'**
> Therefore, if you make a trip to see a friend, and do some business while there, it is unlikely you can claim the whole thing back.

Also, read the section on 'tax dodging' at the end of the chapter.

Equipment

If you buy equipment for your business, you might not be able to claim back the total cost of this in the first year. Instead, you may be able to claim tax relief in the form of 'capital allowances'. Ask the Inland Revenue for their help sheet IR206 on Capital Allowances, or download it from their website **www.inlandrevenue.gov.uk**.

Cars and tax

I have consistently found this one of the most complex tax issues. Basically, the government is not keen on all of us fat cats swanning around in big German cars noising up the neighbours and polluting the environment.

If your business provides you with a car, you will be taxed for this at quite a high rate, which varies depending on age and engine size. It is often far simpler to keep your car private, and pay all the repairs and insurance yourself. Then you can claim back the business mileage you do during the year. A typical mileage rate is 45p a mile. Over the course of the year, this should pay for itself.

> ⚖ **Entrepreneur's Secret: You do not have to buy a flash car to impress clients**
>
> (a) They will hardly ever see it. Mind you,
> *I used to drive an old battered Renault 5, dubbed uncharitably by a friend, 'Bozo the Clown's car'. After one meeting, a client followed me out into the car park. I was horrified. I said good-bye, walked past the car, round the corner, and hid in a bush until he'd gone back into the office before nipping round and driving off.*
> (b) It will make them jealous and worry they are paying you too much.
> *A great mission statement from a design agency: 'Macs not Mercs'.*

Your first company car may not be quite what you anticipated

VAT

> **If your annual turnover is over a certain limit, you generally have to be registered for VAT**

VAT is the Tax on the Value Added at each stage of production. From the mining of the raw material for your product until it reaches the customer, this amount snowballs until the last person holding the parcel has to pay the amount. This is a clever trick of the government, as you are essentially acting as their tax collector.

The main problem with VAT used to be the paperwork and admin, but, all credit to them, the government are doing a lot to simplify this.

VAT is not administered by the Inland Revenue, but by Customs and Excise. For more information call their helpline: 0845 010 9000 or visit www.hmce.gov.uk.

VAT bands

There are four classifications of VAT.

1. The standard rate of VAT (currently 17.5 per cent).

2. There is a special 5 per cent rate for unusual things.

3. Zero-rated for VAT.

4. Exempt from VAT.

Exempt-rated goods include things like selling and leasing property, insurance, post, some training and education services.

Zero-rated goods are essentially those things the government decide are 'good' for us. They include:

- Food (but not 'bad' things like hot prepared food, catering or 'non-essentials' like confectionery).
- Books and magazines (but not 'bad' ones that are full of ads).
- Exports.
- Children's clothing.

The main difference between these two is that if you only deal in exempt goods, you cannot be VAT registered.

As you might imagine, actually defining what is 'good' and 'bad' is not clear cut, and is subject to a fair degree of legal wrangling.

There was a big expensive legal battle as the makers of Jaffa Cakes argued with the Inland Revenue that their products were 'cakes' – so not liable for VAT, and not 'biscuits' which would have been liable for VAT.

The VAT office provides leaflets on this, and continual updates. If you are in anyway unsure, phone them up and ask them (tel: 0845 010 9000). It's important to get this right as if on an inspection the Inland Revenue find you have not been charging VAT on something you should have, they can demand back-dated payments.

Also, be careful about splitting down your service. If we gave a total price for producing and delivering a book, it would be zero-rated. If we charged extra for delivery – we would have to pay VAT on that.

The system

You have to keep your records for six years. If the VAT people are investigating you, they can look back three years.

For retailers making lots of small sales, VAT is more complicated. There are therefore specific schemes set up to help simplify this.

Generally, you will file a VAT return every quarter. You can opt to do it monthly if you are a masochist, anally retentive or if reclaiming tax.

There is a new flat rate scheme if your turnover is below a certain level. Rather than worrying about all your fiddly records and returns, you can just pay a flat rate of VAT as a proportion of your total turnover.

There is also new annual accounting scheme. Below a set turnover level, you can sit down with the VAT people and work out an estimated amount for the year, based on your previous year's return. You then pay this monthly by direct debit, with a balancing adjustment at the end of the year. You can adjust this throughout the year if circumstances change.

You can also opt for cash accounting. This means that you pay and reclaim tax only when you pay or receive cash for something – not when you issue or receive an invoice. This can help cashflow in some businesses.

For information on these, call the Customs and Excise helpline 0845 010 9000

If you make a mistake

The VAT people have tightened up their enforcement with a whole scale of statutory fines for late payment and errors. However, they have a statutory obligation to go a bit easier on small businesses. If you are having problems, or have made a mistake, follow the cardinal rule of business: phone them up and tell them! They will be much more understanding if you admit to genuine problems than if they think you are trying to pull a fast one.

Tax dodging and cash in hand

There is a fine line between playing all the rules in your favour, and breaking them outright.

It is VERY tempting when you start out to treat all income as your own personal cash, and be less than scrupulous in what you report to the taxman. Be careful! I would avoid this for a number of reasons:

You'll get caught: The Inland Revenue has been around for a lot longer than you have, and it is unlikely you will be the first person to have thought of your latest wizard wheeze for tax avoidance. Don't underestimate their ability to track you down.

During Wimbledon, local house owners started to rent out their drives as parking spaces. The Revenue got wise to this. Tax inspectors would walk up and down the street checking who was doing this, looking at adverts in newsagents and local newspapers and asking around. They then checked that the owners were reporting this income in their tax returns.

Similarly, if someone pays you as a freelance, you will need to account for this as it will be on your customers' records, and the Revenue will often follow the chain.

You do not want to come to the attention of the Revenue (if you can possibly help it): An inspection can be a very time-consuming and expensive affair. Generally, this is helped by filing on time, paying promptly, and having figures that do not seem completely out of the ordinary (trust me – they know such things).

It is bad business practice: You need to be disciplined and think long term with your business. There is no point splashing out a large amount of cash one month and buying yourself some nice toys, only to find when things get tight a few months later you have no cash left and go bust. Get into the habit of paying yourself a regular salary, and bonuses when you make a big sale.

Also, the whole point of being self-employed and having money is to have freedom. If you have to spend the whole of your life stressing about your various fiddles and dodges, it defeats the whole purpose.

CHAPTER 22

Staff

Staff

Should I employ someone?

Hiring the first member of staff is a big step for a small business. Typically, you will worry:

1. It's expensive
2. There's too much red tape
3. I can't trust anyone to do the job as well as me.

Expense: Wages will represent a major expenditure. Before committing to a full-time member of staff you should consider outsourcing, freelancers and part-timers. There are tax implications (National Insurance) on hiring staff, but they are not prohibitive.

Red tape: If you are a reasonable and sensible employer, you should not have to worry too much about regulations. The government's Small Business Service has a guide to the regulations on staff (reference RG02), **www.ukonline.gov.uk**. There is also a helpline for new employers 0845 60 70 143, from which you can also obtain a welcome pack.

If you become a member of the Federation of Small Businesses, you will find they also offer a free employment advice line (**www.fsb.org.uk** or telephone 01253 336000).

I can't trust anyone: Far too many small business owners do it all themselves. This is fine if you intend to stay small though you should still look at the alternatives below. For others, you will quickly learn that the more you free yourself up, the faster your business can grow.

These are not excuses to avoid hiring staff.

Alternatives: Outsourcing and freelancers

Before hiring a full-time member of staff, consider the more flexible alternatives.

Outsourcing certain jobs to specialists or freelancers can seem expensive. However, they will often bring a higher degree of expertise. You also must consider your 'opportunity cost' – i.e. how much more you could earn if you were out selling and not driving the delivery van.

The following are some of the areas small businesses can typically outsource:

- **Deliveries:** Unless delivery is a vital stage in strengthening the relationship with your customer, get someone to do it for you.
- **Book-keeping:** (see Chapter 20).
- **Manufacturing:** This can seem a heretical question in a product business, but you must ask yourself – is my real talent in the physical manufacture of each product, or is it more in the originality of the design, packaging or promotion?

McClaggan Smith sell a range of popular China mugs. If you are drinking out of a humorous mug now, have a look at the bottom to see if their name is there.

They used to employ staff to run a pottery kiln making these mugs. However, this gave them huge staff costs, and there were problems with seasonality, quality control and so on. Instead, they outsourced production to a specialist mug supplier and now just seal on the designs and package in-house. Their real talents as a company are spotting talented designers and their network of sales channels.

What to look for in a member of staff

If you are ready to take the plunge, there are two golden rules in looking for an employee:

1. Hire for attitude not aptitude

It is scary taking on staff. As we saw in the Sales chapter, when faced with scary purchases people don't go for the best, they go for the *least worst*. Resist the following scenario:

> *You get a good gut-feeling for someone in an interview, and are really impressed by their can-do attitude. However, they don't have much industry experience. Then an ex-employee from your competitors comes in. OK, they don't interview very well and are a bit lacklustre, but they've got good qualifications, and after all, your competitors hired them...*

Don't do it! Trust your gut instinct!

Bear in mind, you can train most people in most skills fairly quickly. It is nigh on impossible to change someone's attitude. If they are grumpy and negative, they will spread this around your business and customers.

2.   Resist hiring clones of yourself

If you are a buzzy extrovert, it is no surprise that you are going to be tempted to hire other buzzy entrepreneurs you get on with. This can be a real danger to your business.

You need balance in your business. You definitely need starters and salespeople, but you need an equal balance of finishers back in the office to deliver on the promises all your 'yes' people are making.

Look at the problems Enron got into when its finance people started getting sexy and creative.

Where to find good talent

Your potential employee is one of the most significant investments you will make. It's worth taking a bit of time to make sure you get the right person.

You should go about this approach in exactly the same way as you would your sales process.

1. Start with who you know. Ask around friends and family. However, don't just stop here because it is safe and cheap. If you get the wrong person, it will be neither.

2. Approach local enterprise companies, careers offices and the like. They might have placement schemes to help.

3. Be flexible. You can find excellent candidates in groups such as new graduates, women returning to the workplace after having

children, and retired people looking for work. You will be more than rewarded with their dedication and enthusiasm.

A proud new mother brought her baby to an interview. Great, I thought, we are modern and open employers. Then she started breast-feeding halfway through the interview. I sat staring straight into her eyes, not daring to look anywhere else, like a startled rabbit caught in headlights.

4. Keep in touch with your competitors, and in particular their staff.

5. Consider advertising, but don't just go for the obvious choices. If you're looking for a young and lively new member of staff, a local entertainment listings guide might be a better, and cheaper, option than newspapers.

6. Always be looking. If you have a website, have details of whom to contact for job enquiries. Also keep previous CVs – the applicants might be worth keeping in touch with.

♟ Entrepreneur's Secret:
Beware of employing your friends and family

It can be extremely tempting to do this. You think you know them well, it saves you the bother of interviewing and advertising, you can have a good laugh at the same time, you might be helping them out of a boring job.

For a start – it will make them feel devalued. From the moment they walk in the door, in the back of their mind they'll be thinking 'she only employed me because I'm a mate'. You will also have little time for friendly chats like you used to. Think how hard it will be to discipline them if it's not working out.

If you are determined to do this, at least go through a formal interview process, and consider other applicants.

See also 'partnerships' (Chapter 9).

The interview process

 Toolkit: The following form will help you do this. There is a blank version on the website: (www.fromacorns.com)

Job description:	Shop assistant
Person interviewed	Jennifer Hopeful
Attitudes needed:	Friendly and likes working with people
	Reliable – will turn up on time
	Previous shop experience
	Enthusiastic – will muck in
Questions to ask:	What did you enjoy most about your previous job?
	What achievements are you proudest of?
	What aspects of working in a shop would you most enjoy, and which would you find hardest?
	Tell me about a time when you handled a difficult customer
Notes:	

Score out of ten:	Friendly	Enthusiastic	Reliable	Previous experience

Step One: Write a job description. When doing this, resist just listing the *tasks* the person will have to do, instead think of the *attitudes* they will need. If they are going to serve customers in your sandwich shop, a pleasant friendly personality is more important than food handling skills. Conversely, if someone is going to over-see your production process, a close attention to detail is more important than the fact you hit it off with them. Other attitudes to consider are the ability to work under pressure, whether they are self-motivated and not going to need constant attention, and whether they fit with your 'culture'.

Step Two: Prior to the interview think through and write down the questions to ask which will get the person to open up. Like sales, you need open-ended questions such as 'What type of work environ-ment do you like?', 'What aspects of your last job did you most and least enjoy?', 'What type of job would you like to be doing in five/ten years?' If you ask, 'Are you reliable?' only a muppet would say 'No'.

Step Three: The interview. Your objective is to make the inter-viewee feel as comfortable and relaxed as possible. This is not just being 'nice'. You want them to be as natural as possible so you get an accurate picture of what they are like.

Also, bear in mind, if this is a really good potential recruit, you're going to have to sell to them. Spend a bit of time at the start giving them the background to your business and selling them on your vision.

If practical, it can be good to give them a test. In some technical positions, you will want to check that their skills are as good as they say they are. It also gives you a chance to see what they are like in a working environment.

Step Four: Immediately after the interview, sit down and rate the person. It is tempting to go for a generalised impression, so force yourself to go through your form and be objective, giving them a score out of ten for each of their attitudes and aptitudes. Then you can weight them according to how important they are to you.

How to be a good boss

Once you've got good talent in your business, you have to work hard to keep them fired up, and stop them going elsewhere. There are a number of steps to this:

1. Trust them with responsibility

 What is the point in getting a guard dog, and then barking yourself?

One of the hardest and most important tasks in business is delegation. There is no magic secret to it.

A friend's father built up a large and successful retail business with many staff. My friend was over from America with his new wife on a brief holiday. For the two days they spent with his dad, every five minutes there would be a phone call from a staff member checking something trivial like a carpet colour.

Imagine you are watching a staff member serving a customer. They aren't doing it the way you like to do it, so you stride over and do it yourself. By doing this, you have done the job to your satisfaction, and possibly quicker. You have also achieved the following:

- Completely demoralised the person doing the job, and told them you don't have confidence in them.
- Shown them there is no point in them making their own decisions, or taking responsibility for their actions.
- Shown the customer you don't trust your staff (so why should they?).

And who says your way is the right way anyway?

However, if you delegate complete responsibility (rather than just a task), you will find your staff are far more motivated. They will take control of a whole area of the business, completely freeing you up.

My father gave me a great piece of advice that I didn't really understand at first:

 The best is the enemy of the good

If you are obsessed with every job that you and your staff do being perfect, there are so many other brilliant opportunities you will miss out on.

2. Reward them The best rewards aren't always cash. By joining a small and growing business, a person might get more responsibility, experience, recognition, flexibility, variety, training and room to grow than in a large business. This might mean you don't have to pay them as much as your larger competitors.

They should also share in the successes of the business. This can be in the form of an end-of-year bonus or party, a sales commission or even a stake in the business for the best.

3. Talk to them This sounds obvious, but it doesn't always happen. At least every six months, you should have a scheduled chat with each person. This is a chance to talk about how they've done, the areas they might like to improve on, develop or have more training in. It's also a great chance to listen to how they think the business is doing, and areas you should improve.

4. Inspire them

> *If you want to build a ship, don't drum up the men to gather wood, divide the work and give orders. Instead, teach them to yearn for the vast and endless sea. (Antoine de Saint-Exupéry, The Wisdom of the Sands)*

Entrepreneurs can be the best, and the worst people to work for.

By sharing your strong and convincing vision and passion in where you are going you can instil great willingness in others to follow you.

This can almost make up for your impatience, disorganisation, lack of delegation and recognition, unreliability, etc., etc.

When a staff member leaves

It will happen – brace yourself. The first time it happens it will feel like you've been dumped.

> *My first employee left after a grand total of five days for a better-paid job. For the next week or so, I lay awake at night worrying to myself, 'Was it something I'd said? Should I have tried harder?' Finally, I had to draw a line at standing outside his new employer's office wondering what he had seen in them.*

Bear in mind, it may not be your fault. Try to find out exactly why it is so it doesn't automatically happen to the next person. Also, try to get them to leave on good terms. The last thing you want is an ex-employee running around telling people what you got up to at the Christmas party.

CHAPTER 23

Dealing with failure

Dealing with failure

Learn to embrace failure

Being an entrepreneur is about dealing with failure. However, in this country, failure is a dirty word. There are not many books on failure. People seem to view it as a contagious disease that you will catch just by talking about it. It's like the army who won't teach its soldiers how to retreat.

However, you have to face the fact that failure is an inevitable part of the process. As Thomas Eddison, the inventor of the light-bulb said:

> 'Of the 200 light bulbs that didn't work, every failure told me something that I was able to incorporate into the next attempt.'

Failure is part of the creative process, and though it may sound heretical, there are times when failure is good for you and good for your business. Hopefully, most of these failures will just be small ones. But it will be your ability to deal with them, and keep going, that will determine the success of your business.

 Our greatest glory is not in never falling, but in rising every time we fall (Confucius)

The different types of failure

In my mind, barring outright cataclysmic failure involving bailiffs and court appearances, there are three different types of failure:

When your business becomes a vampire

Not all people realise their businesses have failed.

While not making a loss, they are no longer growing in size. The owners are still working 6 days a week, earning less than they would working for someone else. No one wants to buy the business, and they still have their house as security. Without realising it, they no longer own their business – it owns them.

It's not necessarily their fault – you mustn't underestimate the importance of a good idea in the success of your business. Successful serial entrepreneurs recognise this and move on, realising each time you start up, you will be bigger and better from all the lessons you've learnt.

You also have to consider what economists refer to as 'opportunity cost'. The real cost of you working in one business is the increased revenue you could be earning in an alternative one.

When it's time to sacrifice the sacred cow

As a philosophical Danish co-worker once told me – 'You sometimes have to be prepared to sacrifice the sacred cow'. You have to face the fact that one part of your business, which you have sweated many hours into, has no viable long-term future and is actually holding the rest of your business back. When this happens, you have to have the guts to stop this bit and focus on the rest of your company.

The spectacular story of Shell at the start of this book shows how a company went from a 'failed' small antiques shop to the largest retailer in the world.

When it feels like death by a thousand cuts

However, there will be many times when no matter how much you believe in the long-term success of your business, it will feel like you are continually failing.

Perhaps one of your major customers goes bust, a staff member leaves for a better job, you get a break-in, a competitor wins a great piece of work, and you get a bad cold.

Taken individually, these things wouldn't faze you too much. But taken together, the drip, drip, drip of negative feedback starts to drain the water from the well of your self-esteem. One morning you wake up and think 'Sod this for a game of soldiers' and consider packing it all in.

It's at times like this that you need to give your mojo some medicine, as we explore in the next chapter.

CHAPTER 24

Medicine for your mojo

Medicine for your mojo

Polish your dreams

When a mountaineer gets up in the morning, what is the first thing they do? They look up at the summit of the mountain.

If all a mountaineer ever thought about was the long slow slog in front of them each day, they would never leave their tent. They keep going because they are dreaming about the summit.

It's the same in business. If you are clearly focused on your summit, the broken rocks on your daily path will just become an annoyance.

We all have fantastic dreams as children: becoming a racing driver, millionaire, brain surgeon. It's just that along the way, we let go of them.

I'll let you in on a little secret:

> **The people who achieve their dreams are the people who hold on to them**

A young boy called Jim McColl had a dream – to have a chauffeur-driven Bentley. He is now a successful businessman and recently netted £100 million from selling an offshoot of his main company Clyde Blowers. I walked with him out of an event once. Guess what was waiting for him outside?

The problem is that we try to RATIONALISE our dreams and make them 'realistic'. And of course, if they were realistic, they wouldn't be dreams in the first place.

Here are some tips for better 'dreaming':

1. Don't let other people 'rationalise' your dreams for you. I remember someone in my family asking me what I wanted to become. I said an international publishing mogul. My how they laughed. If you're going to tell someone your wildest dreams, tell a complete stranger. Don't share it with the 'McTaggarts of Dundee' (see Chapter 4). They will say 'yes, but...' Little by little, this will erode your dream until there is nothing left.

2. Stop worrying about how you are going to get there. Start off with where you want to end up, and then work backwards from there. Think, 'If I'm going to be a Hollywood director, I'd better start to muck about with a camcorder' rather than 'I'll never make it to Hollywood from Norwich. I'd better settle on doing local wedding videos'.

3. It is NEVER too late. Ray Krok, the founder of McDonald's, started the company in his sixties!

4. Start with a vague sense of what it is you'd love. Then spend time polishing your dream. Add more details to it, and really start to visualise it. Think of the fine details, or what a typical day in your dream life will be like.

As motivational guru Jack Black said to me after a session on strategy: 'A strong dream is always far more effective than a three year scenario plan from an MBA'.

Surround yourself with supporters

Isolation is a terrible problem for entrepreneurs. You are working on your own on a rainy day, and a customer gives you a hard time. Without anyone to share the misery with, it can get too much.

Try to surround yourself with positive people who believe in you. A good source is other people who have started in business. They will understand intimately the problems you are facing, and can share the horror stories. You don't have to meet them physically, just a phone call or an email is enough sometimes when you've got a problem you want to talk through.

You can join an online networking group. There are also many regional networking groups that can help you with this, and often many informal 'curry clubs'. There is a list of support organisations in the appendix: Useful sources of information. If you can't find one – why not start one?

Take a break

Let your philosophy be that of that great modern thinker, Ferris Bueller:

> 'Life moves pretty fast. If you don't stop and look around once in a while, you might miss it'. (Ferris Bueller's Day Off)

 Success is a long hike rather than a quick sprint

There is a real macho tendency with small business owners. Put a group together and soon you'll hear:

> 'I work a ten hour day.' 'Well I work a twelve hour day, and do this six days a week'. 'Oh, that's nothing. I work a twenty hour day, and when I get home, I go for a two hour run and my last holiday was a ten hour break in 1987.'... (Apologies Monty Python)

You simply cannot work fifteen hours a day, six days a week, twelve months a year without (a) becoming a complete basket case or (b) ending up really hating your work. In fact, psychologists have shown you can only really concentrate effectively for forty minutes at a time.

So for goodness sake, give yourself a break! Heed the motto of Ru Paul, a 6ft 6ins former American football star drag queen, who took his philosophy from a motorway sign:

> 'Have space, give space'

It is only when you have created enough room in your own life that you have time to listen and learn from others.

Go for a decent walk at lunchtime, or have a nap. Take holidays when you can even if you have to squeeze them in around work. Don't worry, you're not as irreplaceable as you perhaps like to think you are – your business will still be there when you get back.

Don't be hamstrung by a search for perfection:

> **The greatest trick is not to finish every task, but rather to leave some tasks undone**

Get fit

The Ancient Greeks used to teach a concept called 'kaloskagathos'. They believed you should spend equal parts of your day working and playing sport. Exercise is a great way to get rid of stress at the end of a day, and being fit makes it much easier to handle the pressures of work.

Don't hide under the duvet

If you are having problems, don't retreat under your duvet and refuse to speak to anyone. It may seem like a good short-term strategy, but your problems will not go away. However, you will find that when you confront your problems or mistakes, they are never as bad as you had imagined them.

Also, don't avoid making tough decisions that need to be made. To paraphrase Andy McNab recounting his experience in the Gulf War in *Bravo Two Zero*:

'We may not always have made the right decisions, but the worst decision you can make is not to make any decision.'

Banish negativity

Excessive negativity can eat away at you. If someone says you look ill, in about ten seconds you will start to feel ill. Don't listen to the negative chat of others, and don't indulge in it yourself.

> **♟ Entrepreneur's Secret:**
> If someone asks how you are, don't say 'not bad'. Just say you are 'good'. It is exactly the same thing, but will make you feel far more positive.

Don't be too self-critical: There is an interesting phenomenon in psychology:

> If you ask the witnesses of a road accident to say what caused it, they will cite a whole range of external factors – the weather, light and traffic conditions. If you ask the driver, they will substantially over-estimate their own role in this.

This happens in business. If you are successful, everyone else will be quick to look at all the external factors – you were in the right place at the right time, or you got lucky. If your business goes wrong – your overwhelming tendency will be to overly blame yourself, even if it was really down to external factors.

There are so many factors in making a business successful, and equally so many reasons it can go wrong. If your business doesn't work out, don't worry: it is not the end of the world. As Henry Ford said:

 Failure is only the opportunity to begin again more intelligently

Handling stress

There is a misconception about stress.

Stress is not hard work. Real stress comes from not being in control of your environment.

Short-term stress in your business is not necessarily a bad thing. Having a period of working long hours to tight deadlines can be well worth it if you get a good pay-off.

Long-term stress is the killer. This typically comes from other people having control of major aspects of your life. I actually think being an entrepreneur is one of the least stressful occupations, as you don't have to work for an idiot boss. Yes, it might all go pear-shaped, but at least it's all your fault!

Accept that there is a season for things:

> There is a tide in the affairs of men
> Which taken at the flood, leads on to fortune:
> Omitted, all the voyage of their life
> Is bound in shallows and in miseries.
> (William Shakespeare, Julius Caesar, IV.iii)

Business, like all things in life, goes through seasons. You will grow in fits and starts. When it's busy, you will be wishing the work would go away. And then mysteriously, it does, and you are left wondering where it all went.

This is partly because when you are growing too fast, you are too busy doing the work and not filling your sales funnel with new leads (see Chapter 15). It is also just the way the universe is.

If things are growing like Topsy, don't assume they always will and borrow to the hilt for a new sports car. Conversely, if things are going wrong, accept that this might just be a phase, and success is just around the next corner.

Learn crying as a negotiation technique

The most important commodity you can offer your customers is trust. If you have made a mistake, admit it early, admit it honestly and admit it directly. Research shows customers are more loyal if they have been through a problem period with a supplier which has been successfully resolved. A genuine and heartfelt apology will usually defuse any situation.

When I started off publishing yearbooks, I used to do all the typing myself. Finishing a book late one night, I didn't notice the spell checker had 'corrected' the name of one of the students Angus MacDonald by taking the 'g' out of his first name. I shipped the books off to China and it wasn't until the graduation day that someone spotted the mistake.

I was mortified. I grovelled in humble apology, I offered to reprint the books, I offered to apologise personally to Angus. However, the students just thought it was funny, and let me get away with it.

Don't say: 'at least it can't get any worse', as this will inevitably cause it to do so immediately.

Never say: 'At least things can't get any worse.'

Take a brave pill!

There is no doubt that starting a business is scary, but anything worthwhile in life generally is.

So go on, be bold, and take a brave pill.

I have the following postcard from a colleague sitting on my desk as I write this. It is a quotation from the German philosopher Goethe:

*Until one is committed, there is hesitancy,
the chance to draw back, always
ineffectiveness.*

*Concerning all acts of initiative there is
one elementary truth the ignorance of which
kills countless ideas and endless plans:
the moment you definitely commit yourself,
then Providence moves. All sorts of things
occur that would never otherwise have
occurred. A whole stream of events issue
from the decisions, raising in your favour all
manner of unseen incidents and meetings
and material assistance, which you could
never have dreamed would come your way.*

*Whatever you can do or dream you can,
begin it.*

*Boldness has genius, power and
magic to it.*

Go for it!

Useful sources of information

Bank of Scotland Business Banking

There is a wealth of valuable technical start-up information and templates on the Bank of Scotland Business Banking website: **www.bankofscotland.co.uk/business/startup**, or call 0845 300 1956.

Government support

The Business Links

There are 45 local Business Links operating across England. The Business Link website is where you can find advice about government funding, grants, legislation and starting a business: **www.businesslink.org**.

Scottish Enterprise

In Scotland, a similar service is provided through a network of Local Enterprise Companies. The Business Gateway is a single access point to a range of integrated services for businesses in Scotland. The website details start-up, growth and information services available: **www.bgateway.com**.

Other links

The Small Business Service: **www.sbs.gov.uk**
UK online **www.ukonline.gov.uk**
Support for going online: **www.ukonlineforbusiness.gov.uk**
Inland Revenue: **www.inlandrevenue.gov.uk**
The Patent Office: **www.patent.gov.uk**
The Office of Fair Trading: **www.oft.gov.uk**
Customs and Excise: **www.hmce.gov.uk**

For young people

Prince's Trust and Prince's Scottish Youth Business Trust

Includes a directory of other young people started in business, hints and tips: **www.princes-trust.org.uk** and **www.psybt.org.uk**.

Shell LiveWIRE

Help and advice for 16-30 year olds setting up in business and national business competition: **www.shell-livewire.org**.

Young Enterprise and Young Enterprise Scotland

A unique scheme to encourage and develop enterprise skills in students aged 15-25: **www.young-enterprise.org.uk** and **www.yes.org.uk**.

Junior Chamber of Commerce and Junior Chamber Scotland

A Leadership Development organisation. Develops useful skills in members so that they may excel in everything they do: **www.bjc.org.uk** and **www.jcscotland.org.uk**.

For women

Bank of Scotland Women and Business

Information on support, case studies and statistics on women in business: **www.bankofscotland.co.uk/business/womenandbusiness**.

British Association of Women Entrepreneurs

This is a non-profit professional organisation for UK based women business owners. Founded in 1954, BAWE encourages the personal development of member entrepreneurs and provides opportunities for them to expand their business: **www.bawe-uk.org**.

Scottish Business Women

A real online forum where you can find out about initiatives and events that can give you assistance, and benefit from an information resource that tells it like it is: **www.scottishbusinesswomen.com**.

Business support groups

Federation of Small Businesses

The UK's leading lobbying and benefits group for small businesses. The website contains information concerning the key issues facing the small business sector today: **www.fsb.org.uk**.

Forum of Private Business

The Forum of Private Business (FPB) is a pressure group lobbying for members to change laws and policies for their future benefit. They also offer advice on problems such as red tape, employment law, health and safety and many other issues: **www.fbp.co.uk**.

Entrepreneurial Exchange

Run 'for entrepreneurs by entrepreneurs', the Exchange is Scotland's premier networking group for ambitious, growth oriented entrepreneurs: **www.entrepreneurial-exchange.co.uk**.

British Chambers of Commerce

With 135,000 members, the British Chambers of Commerce comprise a national network of Chambers, uniquely positioned at the heart of every business community in the UK: **www.chamberonline.co.uk**.

Institute of Directors

The (IoD) is the leading membership organisation for directors who are responsible for the strategic direction of companies: **www.iod.com**

What's missing?

To: Caspian Woods
        Editions
        72 Newhaven Road
        Edinburgh EH6 5QG

Or email: **caspian@fromacorns.com**

I think you should add or change the following information in your next book:

_____
_____
_____
_____
_____
_____

I have found the following source of information helpful:

_____
_____
_____
_____
_____
_____

I have the following suggestions to improve your book:

_____
_____
_____
_____
_____
_____

Name: _____
Address (optional): _____
_____
_____

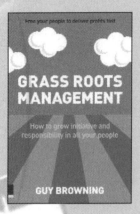

Grass Roots Management

How to grow initiative and responsibility in all your people

Guy Browning
0273662996

Imagine your in-tray full of solutions not problems. Think of your team empowered and actually using its power. Visualise the whole workforce energised from the bottom up. You can make this happen. It's called Grass Roots Management. How to get your people to take the initiative, take responsibility and take the business forward. Fast.

Marketing Judo

Building your business using brains not budget

John Barnes & Richard Richardson
0273 66316X

How to build your business through brilliant marketing – but without a big budget. As in judo, use your brains not brawn, and leverage the weight of your opponent to your advantage. Written by two men who did just that, to make Harry Ramsden's into a multi-million pound business.

Fast Thinking Managers Manual

Working at the speed of life

Ros Jay
0273 652982

It's a fast world with tight deadlines and you squeezed in between. What you need are fast solutions to help you think at the speed of life. This essential manual gives the clever tips and vital information you need to make the best of your last minute preparation. You'll look good. They'll never know.

The Fast Thinking Managers Manual – it is big and it is clever.

Please visit our website at:

www.pearson-books.com

PERSONAL NOTES

PERSONAL NOTES